SHOPS & Boutiques

SHOPS & Boutiques

Foreword by Giorgio Armani

Grant Camden Kirkpatrick AIA

Architecture & Interior Design Library
An Imprint of PBC International, Inc.

Distributor to the book trade in the United States and Canada
Rizzoli International Publications Inc.
300 Park Avenue South
New York, NY 10010

Distributor to the art trade in the United States and Canada
PBC International, Inc.
One School Street
Glen Cove, NY 11542

Distributor throughout the rest of the world
Hearst Books International
1350 Avenue of the Americas
New York, NY 10019

Library of Congress Cataloging–in–Publication Data

Kirkpatrick, Grant.
Shops & boutiques / by Grant Kirkpatrick
    p.   cm.
Includes index.
  ISBN 0–86636–291–6   (pbk ISBN 0–86636–381–5)
  1. Specialty stores—Designs and plans 2. Store decoration—
Psychological aspects.   I. Title. II. Title: Shops and boutiques.
NA6220.K5 1994   94–25806
725' .21—dc20   CIP

CAVEAT– Information in this text is believed accurate, and will pose no problem for the student or casual reader. However, the author was often constrained by information contained in signed release forms, information that could have been in error or not included at all. Any misinformation (or lack of information) is the result of failure in these attestations. The author has done whatever is possible to insure accuracy.

Color separation by Fine Arts Repro House Co., Ltd., Hong Kong
Printing and binding by C&C Offset Joint Printing Co., (HK) LTD., Hong Kong

Printed in Hong Kong

10 9 8 7 6 5 4 3 2 1

this book is dedicated
to my parents Nadine & Bob...
for you are the epitome of dedication

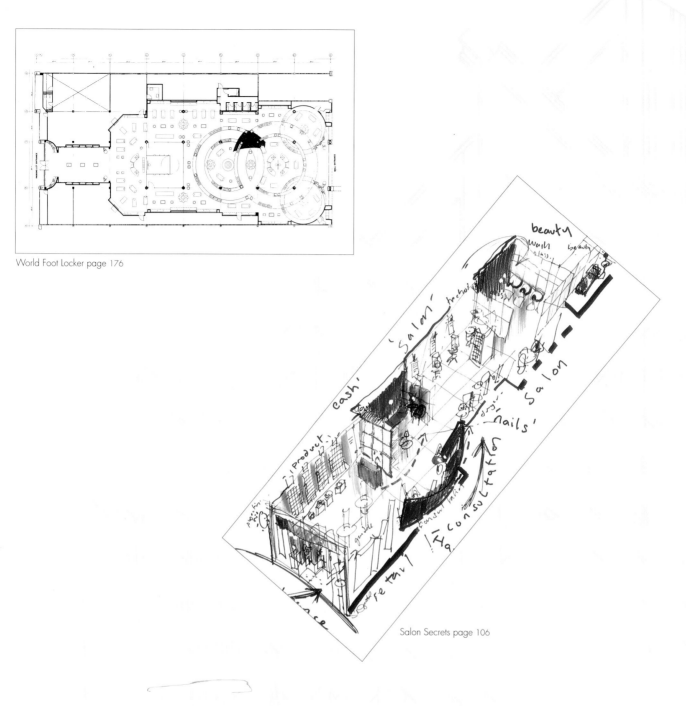

World Foot Locker page 176

Salon Secrets page 106

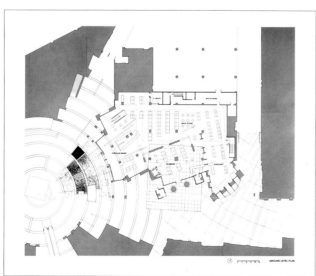

Sam Goody page 20

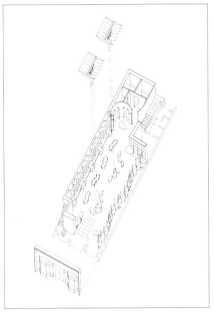

Oasis page 148

Contents

Foreword   *9*
Giorgio Armani

Introduction   *10*
Grant Camden Kirkpatrick AIA

Store Imagery   *12*

Economic Design   *80*

Unconventional Venues   *128*

Appendix   *180*

Index   *182*

Acknowledgments   *184*

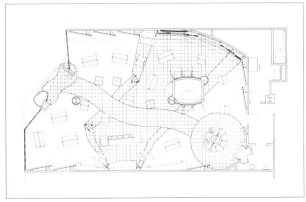

Hanna-Barbera page 66

Foreword

Giorgio Armani

What exactly are the functions of a store? The first and most obvious is to establish contact—more specifically a bond—between the producer and the consumer. Important as this function is, however, it isn't reason enough for putting one's name into the retail marketplace. In reality, a boutique is a superbly effective means of communication through which you establish your trademark, your image, with the public. It becomes your actual calling card. From the moment your name is on a sign and you've displayed your merchandise, from the moment you've made your choice of street, a particular building, even the size of the windows, you reveal a moment of truth. That "truth" lies in how closely you've integrated the product's quality with its presentation.

A designer's boutique must somehow manage to convey both the philosophy and the creative energy that go into developing a collection. The force of that impact can be either enhanced or minimized, depending upon management. For instance, it isn't unusual or rare to find boutiques where even the most insignificant things are exalted or, on the other hand, beautiful things are destroyed. How then, you might ask yourself, can a boutique convey the philosophy and creative energy of a collection. The answer is atmosphere. Atmosphere is composed of two elements—elements that, in my opinion, are key to the success of not only a boutique but a corner in a department store.

Furnishings are the first element. Furnishings must reflect the soul of the product, the brand, as well as create what I call a thousand and one "complicities"—the subtle temptations which lure a consumer into the store for a quick look. If he or she is then captivated by a friendly space, by easy-to-look-at displays and pleasant lighting, the store will be successful. It will be even more successful if the second element of atmosphere is there. I'm talking about the salespeople. Salespeople who, quite apart from being courteous and patient, must also develop a great product sensibility—an awareness. Because the ultimate goal for those who do a job like mine is to communicate with those who buy the product and the feeling.

Introduction

Grant Camden Kirkpatrick AIA

From the agora of ancient Greece to the super-mall of our modern cities, the marketplace occupies a special part of our history and culture. A shopping district for the exchange of goods lies at the heart of each city in every society. The character of each shopping district, whether swap-meet or stock exchange, small town main street or regional mall, grows from the features of its components: the shops.

Each shop is formulated from a multitude of pressures: shifting lifestyle patterns, social and economic conditions, cultural trends, and technological advances. A  kaleidoscope of consumers and products continually fuels the development of new merchandise and the demand for new and innovative environments for the sale of these products. Today's accelerating pace of change poses a special challenge to the store designer. Never before has the relationship between product and environment been more crucial than it is in today's fiercely competitive global marketplace.

Retailers take a vested interest in determining and analyzing what formulates our culture and defines its necessities. In much the same way that merchandise develops in response to social change, the environments in which products are merchandised reflect societal changes as well. New retail venues become forums for experimentation and, as such, contribute to the shaping of our cultural future.

A store's success can be tied to its adaption to the most immediate societal changes and its long-term approach to larger cultural issues. The successful retailer has recognized the importance of store design as an integral component of retailing—shops and boutiques around the world have created or transformed their image and merchandise to respond to the multitude of pressures. In our constantly changing society, the relationship between a store's image and its product is the major challenge to its success.

This book seeks to present progress and ingenuity through the recognition of change in our society

as a design challenge. It is not about what is right or what is wrong in retail design—it does not attempt to expound great wisdom about the rules of proper store design and merchandising. Rather it is a showcase for innovative retail design and the many ways in which talented designers and store owners across the globe have solved a series of complex issues and challenges in creating environments that enhance the sale of their products in the context of a changing society.

Architects and designers are influenced by broad issues that serve as a backdrop to the design process. These include cultural practices, local and global economics, and the competition engendered by free enterprise. No less important, basic retail challenges of display, circulation, and lighting figure in this process also. In the pages that follow, you will see stores that have all successfully addressed these basic retail issues. Yet these stores have formulated their unique retail environments with innovative answers to the broader issues outlined above.

Organized into three thematic sections, *Shops & Boutiques* features a select palette of recently built stores from around the world. Instead of grouping the projects according to their contents, I have chosen to highlight certain family resemblances. These resemblances derive from the manner in which these shops and boutiques have created or transformed their image to more closely associate with the way people live their lives—Store Imagery; perceive value—Budget Design; and conduct their shopping—Unconventional Venues. Clearly each store has several design challenges and solutions, and thus, some relate to more than just one category. But each maintains a dominant design concept— a resemblance derived from the kind of solution to a particular problem type that formulated its success and uniqueness.

Store Imagery displays projects that directly adapt the image of their target customer and merchandise to the architectural space. With examples of famous designers' stores, department store boutiques and innovative projects for new retail chains, *Store Imagery* focuses on the successful relationship between a product and its retail context.

Economic Design displays projects from all over the world which respond to a truly timeless and universal design parameter, the

budget, as a challenge to lead to the most playful and creative solutions. From high fashion designer boutiques on a diet, to small, value-conscious stores, *Economic Design* seeks the most creative solutions to the most common design limitation.

Unconventional Venues attends to projects whose integration of special features or additional uses have created spaces that attract customer attention or emotion without regard to "standard" retail store layout. From mini-department stores to mixed-use retail showrooms, *Unconventional Venues* presents retail environments that have successfully pushed the envelope of the shopping experience.

As readers browse through this compendium of retail ingenuity, it is my hope that they will note the indi-vidual circumstances and efforts that have contributed to the success of each store...to view each one within its own

set of challenges and to recognize the creativity that ultimately makes these stores a contribution to society, the marketplace and our individual inspiration.

Store Imagery

Today's lifestyles and social values are represented in an almost superrealistic way in many new retail venues, and stores have quickly realized that their image can be critical to the customer's total shopping experience. Stores create imagery through an emulation of their environment and products, to project their image and perceived product value, and to elicit memories and emotions about familiar products.

A few bold new stores have created imagery that is synthesized from current needs and lifestyles resulting from complex issues in our society, such as the decentralization of our urban cores and their resulting fragmented neighborhoods. Urban Outfitters in Santa Monica, California, and Anthropologie in New York City respond to their urban context and eclectic product mix with a distressed and "broken" palette of materials simulating the familiar haven of the consumer. Because of the broad range of merchandise, the designs seek to fuse the environment and appeal to a variety of sensibilities.

Many retailers create an image that becomes the trademark for their product and name. These stores often seek a high-end design context for the sale of their merchandise to create an environment that reinforces the worth of their product. Famous retail names such as Giorgio Armani, Bergdorf Goodman, and Barneys New York work with top designers to create showcase store environments, treating every detail of design with the same creativity and uniqueness that makes their merchandise a household name.

With the increasing popularity of entertainment merchandising, many designers have created store imagery that directly emulates the product. Hanna-Barbera, Caesar's World, Looney Tunes, and Sam Goody infuse their shoppers with lively environments showcasing their colorful characters and products, and interactively involving the customer with hands-on exhibits and merchandise display.

Banana Republic

Retail Clothing/Specialties

Beverly Hills, California

The new West Coast flagship store for Banana Republic in Beverly Hills, California was a direct response to the relationship between store imagery and product. Banana Republic, owned by the GAP corporation, was attracted to the building by the significant character of the original 1920s interpreted and eclectic Mediterranean style. A featured outdoor entry vestibule, limestone surrounds, and cherry wood windows combine to give the building a warmth and character that simulates the store's merchandise. The attraction for the store's clientele begins on the street and continues through to the interior spaces.

The interior of the 8,000 square foot store is dominated by a double sided scissor stair within a large skylit vestibule. The comfortable and semi-casual clothing product is displayed within a relaxed and residential-like environment with a seating group around a stone fireplace, and several custom display fixtures incorporating antique doors and gates with new iron bases and glass tops. Materials such as wood and limestone floors and cotton drapes with belt buckle tiebacks complete the soft ambiance.

Owner/Company
GAP, INC.

Building Owner
BRUCE MEYER

Architects/Designers
KIRKPATRICK ASSOCIATES
ARCHITECTS, AIA
AVILA & TOM COMPANY

Interior
ROBERT ENGEL

Lighting Designers
GRENALD ASSOCIATES, LTD.

Structural Engineer
RMJ

General Contractor
FISHER DEVELOPMENT, INC.

Photographer
SHARON RISEDORPH

Banana Republic

Apparel

New York, New York

In the ultimate example of store design bringing merchandise and imagery together, GAP, INC. Store Planning, the in-house designer for the new Banana Republic at 85th and Madison in New York, describes the result as "designing and merchandising by environments."

The store's upscale atmosphere is a response to its location on New York's Upper East Side. Each of the store's seven specialized departments has adopted an individual aesthetic to closely associate with the merchandise on display. The departments are described as "rooms" which temporarily absorb the shopper in a comfortable, almost residential atmosphere. To reinforce this boutique-like intimacy, the spaces have various ceiling heights, furniture and fixtures, but they retain a cohesive theme by sharing a common palette, tile floor pattern, and finish casework.

The warmth and character of the signature Banana Republic clothing is reflected in the details of the store as well. Custom fixtures including mosaic tile tables, steel and wood display units, and layout tables made of antique bases with slabs of honed marble and granite provide focal points and sales surfaces in the individual environments and circulation spaces. Original artwork, antique mirrors, and contemporary furniture complete the eclectic imagery and provide for the practical needs of the shopper.

Owner/Company
GAP, INC.

Architect/Designer
GAP, INC. STORE PLANNING

Lighting Designer
GRENALD ASSOCIATES, LTD.

Contractor
FISHER DEVELOPMENT

Photographer
WILLIAM WALDRON

Sam Goody

Prerecorded Music

Universal City, California

Owner/Company
SAM GOODY

Architects/Designers
THE MUSICLAND GROUP, INC.
THE JERDE PARTNERSHIP, INC.

Principal
JON JERDE, FAIA

Senior Associate Designer
RICHARD ORNE, AIA

Project Team
DAVID GLOVER, JOHN LEGGITT

Project Designers
JEFF DEYOE, MICHAEL MATHEWS

Project Manager
ROBERT WOELFFER, AIA

Architects of Record
THE MUSICLAND GROUP, INC.

Environmental Graphic Designer
BILL MURPHY & COMPANY

Signage Designer
OLIO

Signage Fabricator
SUPERIOR

Structural Engineer
MARTIN & ASSOCIATES

MEP Engineers
W.J. SUTHERLAND & ASSOCIATES

Acoustics and Media Technologies
SMITH, FAUSE & ASSOCIATES

Lighting Designer
JOE KAPLAN ARCHITECTURAL
LIGHTING

Contractor
PACIFIC SOUTHWEST
DEVELOPMENT, INC.

The synthesis of three distinct merchandising departments for the new Sam Goody store at the Universal Citywalk exhibits a design of dynamic expression by the Jerde Partnership design team.

The new building sits on the center court of an outdoor shopping mall in Southern California. Representing the three merchandising concepts of Sam Goody, the design pronounces each area through unique and interrelated façades. The customer enters the Popular Music department through an animated, neon-accented color plaster façade. The entrance to the Classics department and the upstairs Coffee Cafe is between two 40 foot high, 10 foot in diameter Corinthian columns within an interpretative classical façade. A 35 foot high, two-dimensional profile sign depicting King Kong climbing the face of a black and metallic bronze tile building hangs over the entrance to Suncoast Motion Picture Company (video).

The central sales environment is referred to as Backstage, and has the character and atmosphere of a soundstage/studio. The two-story space is defined by upper level catwalks and the destination mezzanine known as the Coffee Cafe. A three-dimensional, walk-through Media Wall features music advertising, photos, oversized images, photo lightboxes, video monitors, projected music videos, reader boards and graphic elements.

Media events are orchestrated throughout the day in an ever-changing environment that depicts the trends of popular music and movies. Weather reports, current events and promotional messages continuously scroll by on the reader boards. In-store performances, CD signings and record promotions bring a sense of "an event" to the store. A live VJ/DJ controls all aspects of the store's music and video media, and interacts with the customers.

On a floating piano-shaped level, the Classics department features a state-of-the-art inventory of classical and jazz selections and creates a controlled, intimate area for the customer with special acoustics, localized sound systems, listening stations and lighting. In the Suncoast Motion Picture Company department, tall video columns accent the environment, supporting the sale of videos and laserdiscs. Interspersed throughout the department are video monitors creating the effect of video confetti. The Coffee Cafe features a wide variety of interactive listening stations and media experiences. It is intended to be an intimate environment where the customer can pause, enjoy the fare, engage in conversation and take in views of the store as well as the street below through its windows.

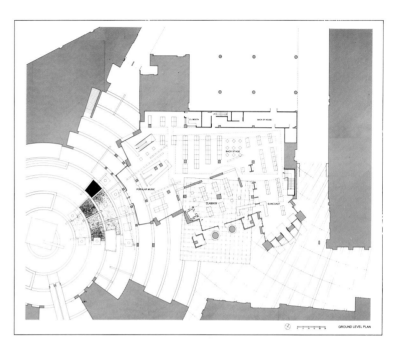

GROUND LEVEL PLAN

25

Barneys New York

Apparel/Accessories

Troy, Michigan

With a single grand gesture, Rosenblum/Harb Architects created an inviting solution for the two-story, 19,000 square foot space designed for Barneys New York in Troy.

The street level women's department and second level men's store are connected by a grandly proportioned staircase. The intricate railing detail of polished stainless steel, sandblasted steel and glass is echoed in the architect designed fixtures and furnishings throughout the store. The custom display fixtures feature a variety of exotic wood veneers, etched glass and custom-crafted steel, bronze, and nickel-plated metal work.

Utilizing selected early modern display fixtures and furnishings in conjunction with the specially designed fixtures, Barneys New York evokes an eclectic and sophisticated palette that caters to both their male and female customers.

Owner/Company
BARNEYS NEW YORK

Architect/Designer
ROSENBLUM/HARB ARCHITECTS

Lighting Designer
JOHNSON SCHWINGHAMMER

Contractor
RICHTER & RATNER CONTRACTING

Photographer
PAUL WARCHOL PHOTOGRAPHY

Barneys New York

Apparel/Accessories

Dallas, Texas

Rosenblum/Harb Architects were greeted with a variety of design challenges, programmatic requirements, and a palette of eclectic merchandise for the new Barneys New York store in Dallas, Texas.

The 20,000 square foot exclusive retail clothing store houses several departments featuring a variety of goods and services including men's and women's clothing, jewelry/accessories, housewares, and an apothecary. A hair salon and restaurant complete the full shopping experience for the Barneys customer.

An eclectic approach to the overall design accommodates the different attitudes of the departments. The hair salon was designed with utilitarian minimalism, the restaurant simulates its food with a Tuscan motif, and the retail departments

Owner/Company
BARNEYS NEW YORK

Architect/Designer
ROSENBLUM/HARB ARCHITECTS

Lighting Designer
JOHNSON SCHWINGHAMMER

Contractor
RICHTER & RATNER CONTRACTING

Photographer
PAUL WARCHOL

take on a museum-like contemporary backdrop to pronounce the sophisticated merchandise within. These distinctive retail departments include an Armani Shop, Chelsea Passage, and a Donna Karan Boutique.

Materials and finishes were selected to emphasize the varied departments including glass and stone mosaic tile, specially painted surfaces, murals, and custom casework and fixtures throughout. Antiques from the 1920s and '30s were incorporated in the contemporary spaces to emphasize the eclectic product base.

Rēvo

Sunglasses

Aspen, Colorado

Echoing a growing sentiment of today's retail store, Rēvo asked Holey Associates of San Francisco to create a display atmosphere that invites the customer to pick up and touch the product—Rēvo's new high-quality line of sunglasses.

Located in the Rocky Mountain setting of Aspen Colorado, Rēvo's first retail store combines a rich palette of materials in a simple setting that educates the customer about their products and technology. Rēvo requested an innovative visual presentation of the entire product line, performed in part by an angled sycamore paneled display wall as the backdrop for the metal display pedestals. The angle of the wall and lighting techniques draw the customer to the product and lead the eye to the cylindrical transaction area for purchases.

To encourage the customer to experience the merchandise, the designer created display pedestals of hammer-tone metal and inset mirrors, echoing the advanced technology intrinsic to the client's product line. Completing the palette for the 600 square foot store are slate floors, leather seating, and custom designed display islands utilizing the same accessible and inviting materials.

Owner:
RĒVO, INC.

Architect:
HOLEY ASSOCIATES

Lighting Designer:
HOLEY ASSOCIATES

Graphic Designer:
CLEMENT MOK DESIGNS, INC.

Millworker:
HEARTWOOD

General Contractor:
ROCKY MOUNTAIN
CONSTRUCTION, INC.

Photographer:
JOHN SUTTON PHOTOGRAPHY

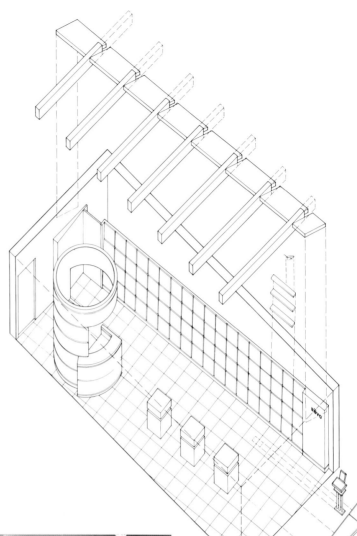

Anthropologie

Specialty Apparel/Accessories/Furniture

Wayne, Pennsylvania

Anthropologie's eclectic merchandise prompted Pompei A.D. to design a site-specific environment for a store that wouldn't "feel like a store."

A 1930s historic warehouse building became the preferred environment in which to mix the range of styles, cultures and materials inherent in the merchandise. The deco terra cotta façade was refurbished and pierced with a contemporary plate glass window system. The juxtaposition of old and new is carefully fused to appeal to different sensibilities represented by a variety of customers.

Inside, the warehouse character is reinforced with an open 6,500 square foot retail space of exposed structural trusses, brick walls, and mechanical systems. The center floor area uses planks salvaged from an old barn and contains a foyer of cracked glass, an oval fountain of cracked tile, and fixtures made of bark-covered tree trunks. One side of the retail space is organized into individual vignettes displaying bedroom and dining room furnishings. It also contains an espresso bar and a cash wrap desk made of galvanized metal and copper wire. Materials such as natural, aged woods, and metals with oxidized patinas were selected based on their tactile qualities.

Owner/Company
URBAN OUTFITTERS

President
RICHARD HAYNE

Creative Director
SUE OTTO

Architect/Designer
POMPEI A.D.

Design Principal
RON POMPEI

Landscape Architect
LAUREL HILL GARDENS

Custom Fixture Fabricator
CHANDLER AND PATON

Custom Wall Finishes
OTTO INDUSTRIES

Graphic Designer
URBAN OUTFITTERS

Photographer
© TOM CRANE

Mossimo Supply

Apparel/Accessories

Costa Mesa, California

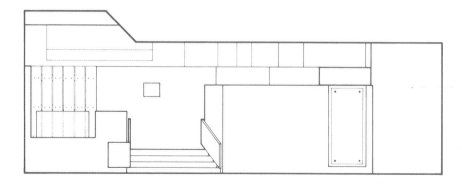

Schweitzer BIM created a unique environment to display Mossimo Supply's rapidly expanding clothing and accessories line by emphasizing the store location's inherent disadvantages.

The designer was faced with two significant challenges; in addition to being located on the top floor of the mall, the original shell space was 2 feet above the adjacent mall level. The combination of these typically terminal retail challenges provided an opportunity to appeal to the shoppers' curiosity.

The storefront is pulled-back into the lease space creating an outdoor transition area. Views into the store are through high glass openings, and no merchandise is visible from the outside. This unexpected obstacle heightens the shoppers' curiosity and generates a yearning for a glimpse of what lies beyond.

Owner/Company
MOSSIMO GIANNULLI

Architect/Designer
SCHWEITZER BIM

Lighting Designer
SCHWEITZER BIM

Contractor
ANDERSON CONSTRUCTION

Photographer
© 1994 ANDREW BUSH

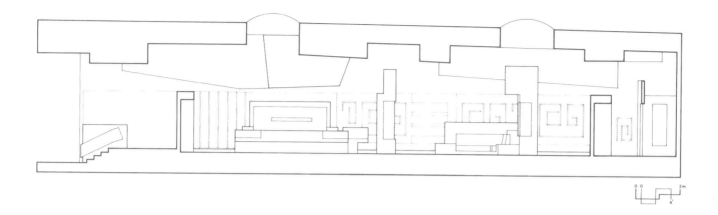

Taking advantage of the top floor location, the designers created a complex ceiling design by combining sculptured ceiling forms with skylights. The design mirrors the movement of the shoppers and also defines high- and low-ceilinged display areas. Organizing the merchandise primarily on the perimeter store walls reinforces the dynamic of the playful ceiling forms and diverse display areas.

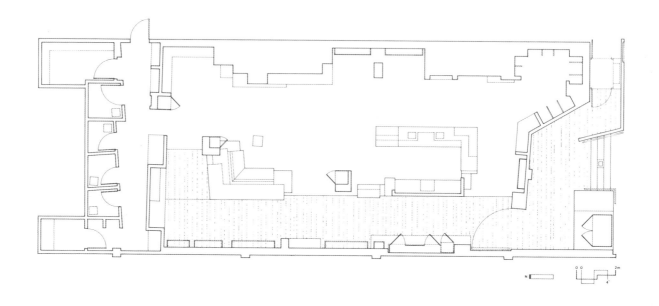

Caesar's World

Gift Shop

Las Vegas, Nevada

With a desire to become the premiere marketer of souvenir merchandise, Caesar's world challenged TSL Merchant Design Group to create a store to emphasize their gaming, sports, and entertainment events in their first venture outside the casino environment.

Three interior areas, each with its own theme, comprise the store. The design starts with the The Forum Mall's traditional Greco-Roman architecture and then unfolds into a whimsical expression of Caesar's image. The first stop on the customer's journey displays high-end fashion and is decorated with oversized dice, gaming chip display fixtures, and a roulette wheel terrazzo floor. Next, the customer moves into souvenir apparel where playing card fixtures and a vignette of Caesar mid-air on a motorcycle recall past Caesar's events. Gaming and boxing memorabilia are sold in the third area— a smoldering depiction of the Roman Coliseum.

Owner/Company
CAESAR'S WORLD

Architect/Designer
TSL/MERCHANT DESIGN GROUP

Designer
RICHARD LEWIS, FISP

Lighting Designer
PASCOE

Store Fixture
STANDARD CABINET

Theming
PANATOM

Photographer
DEREK RATH

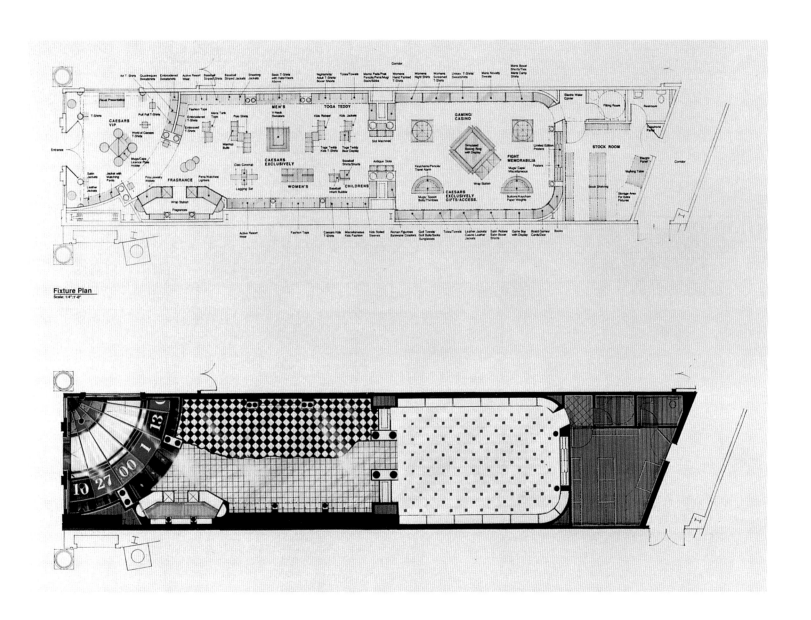

Fixture Plan
Scale: 1/4":1'-0"

The MoMA Design Store

Museum Store

New York, New York

Working with a "less is more" attitude, designers HTI/Space Design International created a museum-like atmosphere for the sale of modern design products from the Museum of Modern Art in New York City.

Inspired by the leaders of the modern movement in architecture, including Mies van der Rohe, Walter Gropius and Le Corbusier, the design team fashioned a retail environment that upholds the principles of the museum responsible for pioneering this movement. Located across the street from the museum, this 3,000 square foot store was intended to be accessible to the many rather than the few. Most merchandise is available for customer handling.

Owner/Company
MUSEUM OF MODERN ART

Architect/Designer
HTI/SPACE DESIGN INTERNATIONAL

Lighting Designer
DAVID APFEL. HTI/SPACE DESIGN INTERNATIONAL

Color Consultant
DONALD KAUFMAN

Photographer
PETER PAIGE

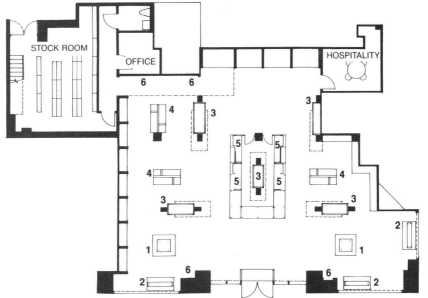

FURNITURE
1 CENTRAL DISPLAY TABLE
2 SHOW WINDOW DISPLAY TABLE
3 CENTRAL DISPLAY CASE
4 ADJUSTABLE SHELVING DISPLAY
5 REGISTER DISPLAY COUNTER
6 CUSTOM SLAT-WALL DESIGN

To carry out the design concept, a sleek, unadorned, architectural setting was created, articulated by slabs of intersecting vertical and horizontal planes that establish the floor plan's grid. Vertical planes are sheathed in panels of light wood and incorporate transparent showcases for merchandise. Freestanding fixtures are used to suggest the museum-like display and facilitate flexible circulation so shoppers can view the objects from different sides as they would a piece of sculpture. An understated approach is reinforced by careful attention to museum-quality lighting, a refined mix of materials including light woods and brushed stainless steel, and a subtly graded paint scheme involving numerous shades of white.

Reflecting MoMA's position as a leader in the sale of modern design products, the store has a restrained and refined atmosphere that serves a clientele with a sophisticated appreciation of design.

Vasari

Apparel/Accessories

Las Vegas, Nevada

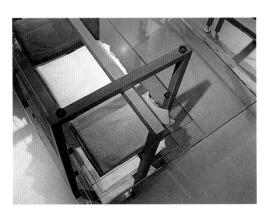

Seeking to continue the evolution of the San Francisco based retailer's identity, Vasari chose Jensen & Macy Architects to design their new store in Las Vegas.

The challenge was to create an environment that would allow the senses to fully appreciate Vasari's avant-garde collection of men's and women's designer clothing and accessories. The designers played upon the unusual shape of the leased space, maximizing display areas to invite exploration, and providing the staff with unobstructed visual surveillance of the products.

The display system, tables, sliding doors, sales counter, and other elements are combinations of simple materials including walnut, steel, gold and silver anodized aluminum, glass, black oxide and brass fasteners. Warm, earthy tones cover the walls, accented by a light blue ceiling, and an integral grey waxed concrete floor. Linear lighting and mechanical systems provide economy and flexibility.

Owner/Company
ARDAVAN NAJMABADI

Architect/Designer
JENSEN & MACY ARCHITECTS

Graphic Designer
JENSEN & MACY ARCHITECTS

Lighting Designer
JENSEN & MACY ARCHITECTS

Photographer
ALAN WEINTRAUB PHOTOGRAPHY

Looney Tunes U.S.A.
Gift Shop

Arlington, Texas

Located in the Six Flags Over Texas theme park, the Looney Tunes concept store, designed by Space Design International, sets its customer in the middle of an animated world.

Shopping becomes a form of entertainment as the store design and merchandise evoke a flood of memories of favorite Looney Tunes cartoons. The 6,000 square foot store is home for a broad array of branded merchandise featuring the famous characters Bugs Bunny, Daffy Duck, Road Runner, Elmer Fudd, Porky Pig, Wile E. Coyote, Sylvester, Tweetie Bird, Speedy Gonzales and others. The variety and complexity of the images—made up of bold colors, wacky perspectives, trompe l'oeil murals, and two- and three-dimensional characters—entice customers to spend more time exploring the different displays.

Owner/Company
SIX FLAGS OVER TEXAS

Architect/Designer
SPACE DESIGN INTERNATIONAL

Graphic Designer
STEVE GROSS, SPACE DESIGN INTERNATIONAL

Lighting Designer
DAVID APFEL, SPACE DESIGN INTERNATIONAL

Photographer
PAUL BIELENBERG

Each of the store's three rooms is decorated in a different cartoon environment. The first room is a theater since the plots of many of the cartoons find the characters performing on stage. A typical home where Tweetie Bird and Sylvester might horse around and get into trouble is the theme of the second room where children's apparel and toys are on display. Higher-end merchandise occupies the third room, decorated with a desert motif out of a Wilie E. Coyote and Road Runner cartoon.

Urban Outfitters

Apparel/Accessories/Housewares

Santa Monica, California

Pompei A.D.'s latest design for the Urban Outfitters stores creates imagery by "fusing urban energy with youthful sensibility," according to owner Richard Hayne.

Located on the Third Street Promenade in Santa Monica, California, the 12,000 square foot store is an adaptive re-use of an original 1927 structure. A trademark of Urban Outfitters stores, the selective demolition of the existing surfaces revealed the building's history. To create the store's signature loft look, layers of

Owner/Company
URBAN OUTFITTERS

President
RICHARD HAYNE

Creative Director
SUE OTTO

Architect/Designer
POMPEI A.D.

Design Principal
RON POMPEI

Custom Fixture Designer
POMPEI A.D.

Visual Merchandiser
SUE OTTO

Fixture Fabricator
CUTWATER BLUE, INC.

Contractor
A.P.C. CONSTRUCTION

Photographer
© TOM BONNER '93

dropped ceilings were removed to reveal the original wood trusses, steel beams and masonry. Patches of plaster, with old wallpaper remaining, are left over the exposed brick walls, and salvaged plywood forms wall sculptures. The lower level, formerly an unused basement, connects to the ground floor by a massive steel stairway. Skylights and industrial halide pendant lights installed in the ceiling emphasize the urban environment.

The 75 foot long street façade was removed and replaced with a steel and wood structure, and plate and broken-tempered glass. Inside, men's and women's casual apparel, accessories, and housewares are displayed with everyday props, including old wooden barrels and tables, custom designed racks, and flea market finds.

Techsis

Design Products

San Francisco, California

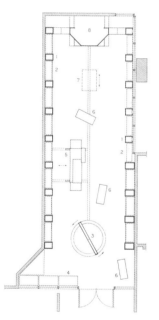

Not unlike the objects it displays, Techsis, designed by Jensen & Macy Architects, is a flexible, machine-like environment created for a constantly changing product line of objects of style, function, and technology.

A series of display mechanisms becomes the "kit of parts" for the store. This collection of adaptable elements forms a kinetic atmosphere for the display and storage of products that share metamorphosis with style and technology. The mechanisms include a revolving glass display slab, telescoping glass tables, a rolling cash desk, display carts, and hanging displays. All pieces are mobile and/or adjustable providing endless possibilities of creative product displays to entice customers.

Perimeter lockable storage pilasters alternate with display bays on the edges of the store. A revolving display slab in the front of the store connects to a beam trolley hanging display system that ends in an elevated rear management office. The office has a bay window for privacy and control.

Utilizing a palette of bleached maple, aluminum, glass and silk-screened fabric, all surfaces and display systems in the 720 square foot store were custom designed and manufactured for maximum flexibility.

Owner/Company
STEFANO PAGLIAI

Architect/Designer
JENSEN & MACY ARCHITECTS

Lighting Designer
JENSEN & MACY ARCHITECTS

Contractor
JAN PEARCE

Photographer
© CHRISTOPHER IRION

Falabella
Department Store
Santiago, Chile

Recognizing store identity as a critical component for attracting customers, the Fitch design team used creative imagery to "connect" the Falabella department store to the new, one million square foot Alto las Condes shopping mall in Santiago.

The four-level, 100,000 square foot store was divided into distinct product categories, each with individual identities. Level one houses perfumes, menswear, and sports and fashion for younger men. Level two contains womenswear, fashion for younger women and childrenswear. Level three is dedicated to housewares and customer services, and level four is occupied by offices and stock rooms. Full-height walls divide the spaces within the levels which feature entrance statements made by large-scale display prints, sets, and abstract photographic panels.

Owner/Company
FALABELLA

Architect/Designer
FITCH

Project Director
GILES MARKING

Design Director
SARA O'ROURKE

Designers
BRUCE SHEPHARD, KRYSTINA KACZYNSKI, ALMUDENA DE TORO

Graphic Designer
GLYNN PHILIPS

Lighting Designer
THEO KONDOS ASSOCIATES

Photographer
JORGE BRANTMEYER

The entry to Falabella from the mall is via the cosmetics hall and dramatic atrium beyond. Featuring specially designed display units that link the different cosmetic brands while retaining brand identity, the cosmetics hall serves as a link to the core of the store—the dramatic four-story skylit atrium. A colored glass wall and floating escalators rise through the atrium to beckon the shopper to the upper levels. Fitch used subtle lighting techniques, color, and materials to emphasize the daylight filtering through to the cosmetics hall below.

Hanna-Barbera

Gift Shop

Los Angeles, California

Seeking to unite shopping and entertainment into one experience, Great American Broadcasting Company hired Space Design International to incorporate the whimsical and familiar world of Hanna-Barbera's best loved cartoon characters into a shopping fantasyland.

The 2,800 square foot store carries a wide variety of Hanna-Barbera's signature merchandise including toys, games, clothing for children and adults, books, audio and video, artwork, and novelties. To house this branded merchandise, the designers created a retail and entertainment environment that captures the spirit of Hanna-Barbera's animated cartoons in sight, sound and motion.

The contemporary design unites Hanna-Barbera's two most popular cartoon families. Prehistoric elements from the Flintstones' world are juxtaposed with futuristic gadgetry from the Jetsons' universe.

Owner/Company
GREAT AMERICAN BROADCASTING
COMPANY

Architect/Designer
SPACE DESIGN INTERNATIONAL

Graphic Designers
KIRAN RAJBHANDARY, LISA THOMAS,
SPACE DESIGN INTERNATIONAL

Photographer
PAUL BIELENBERG

The entrance façade combines boulders from Bedrock, the Flintstones' home town, with a space-age antenna direct from the Jetsons' Orbit City. Inside, customers follow an undulating center aisle which guides shoppers through the various departments, eventually leading them to the interactive video jukebox in the back.

With its bright colors, playful imagery, and wacky humor, the store provides a convincing and familiar arena to entertain both child and adult.

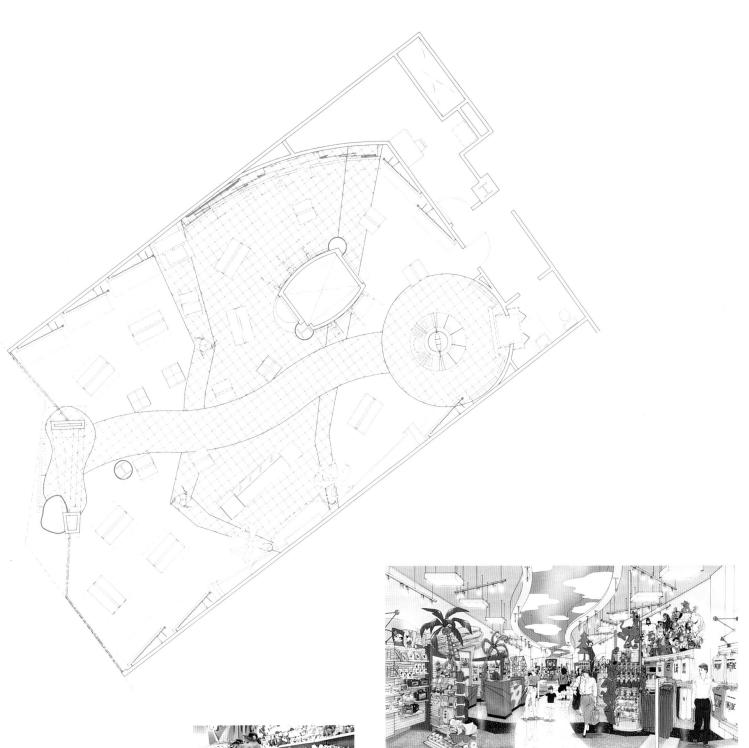

Doral Jewelers

Jewelry

New York, New York

Echoing the precious nature of its merchandise, Doral Jewelers in New York, designed by Dorf Associates, displays its wares in a crafted environment rich in quality materials and detail.

The 15 foot wide by 26 foot deep space comprises a relatively large inventory of jewelry in addition to a walk-in safe, small office, store, and bathroom facilities. The designers managed to create enough mezzanine space to locate the office and storage above, thereby maximizing the selling space and cash/wrap area on the ground floor. A symmetrical layout is reinforced by the vaulted and burnished Chemetal ceiling over the two-story sales area.

Materials used include German greenstone with light-colored limestone and mother-of-pearl inserts. Maple display cases are accented with a green-pigmented stain to match the floor. The Chemetal ceiling and cut glass accents combine with custom-cut textured pendant fixtures to create rich metaphors for the fine-crafted jewelry within.

Lining the perimeter of the store are linear prismatic cut-glass strips illuminated by color-corrected fluorescent cove lighting that provides necessary ambient light. Custom-designed, low-voltage, 50-watt MR-16 pendant fixtures are suspended from the arched ceiling to provide a highlight for attracting potential customers in from the street. The floor and wall cases are illuminated by color-corrected fluorescent lamps, supplemented by vertical low-voltage accent lighting.

Architect/Designer
DORF ASSOCIATES INTERIOR DESIGN INC.

Lighting Designer
MARKUS EARLEY LIGHTING

Contractor
COLUMBIA ART

Photographer
MASAO UEDA PHOTOGRAPHY

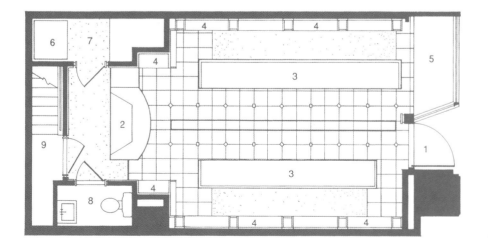

Bergdorf Goodman Men

Men's Apparel/Accessories

New York, New York

Remodeling a Depression-era high-rise into a vanguard luxury store that would uphold Bergdorf Goodman's image of European grandeur and quiet elegance was the challenge brought forth for the J. T. Nakaoka Associates Architects design team.

The store was designed to be an alluring equal to the main Bergdorf Goodman women's store across the infamously busy Fifth Avenue shopping street. The image was to convey confidence, masculinity, understatement and a residential feel. The unique boutique retailing concept of Bergdorf Goodman required almost one hundred distinct shop spaces—contrary to the nonboutique traditional shopping style of most male shoppers.

Owner/Company
BERGDORF GOODMAN

Architect/Designer
J. T. NAKAOKA ASSOCIATES ARCHITECTS

Paint Consultant
DONALD KAUFMAN COLOR

Lighting Design
CRAIG ROBERTS ASSOCIATES, INC.

Contractor
HERBERT CONSTRUCTION COMPANY

Photographer
JAIME ARDILES-ARCE

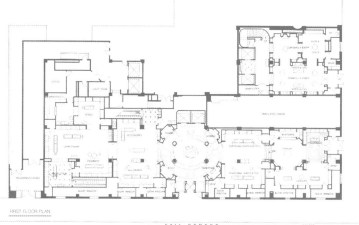

FIRST FLOOR PLAN

58th STREET

Although the sales area totals 40,000 square feet (divided among the building's first three floors), the ground floor provides only 10,000 square feet of usable space. The introduction of a new two-story oval rotunda addressed the spatial difficulties by becoming the ordering point within the floor plan for the six major departments. The rotunda also provides immediate visual access to the second level and serves as a reference point to customers.

The store's layout provides vistas where merchandising presentation is always center stage. The traditional residential architectural vocabulary of vestibules, foyers, rotundas and rooms was used to plan/prioritize dissimilar spaces. Defined aisles were eliminated to visually enlarge otherwise small spaces and increase the transition from one boutique setting to another.

The budget and schedule for the interiors dictated surfaces of mostly drywall with creative painting and adhesive-mounted flexible mouldings. The rotunda dome is custom, but is simple cast gypsum. Marble is used sparingly and the ceiling work is simple and straightforward. Over 50 subtle shades of light, muted grey-beige paint were used to achieve the interior's sophisticated palette. In some instances, as many as 12 to 16 pigments were blended to create a single color.

THIRD FLOOR PLAN   58th STREET

Economic Design

The retail industry is dependent on the status of its economic base and the perception of value by its customers. Therefore, store owners are often challenged to create and promote their sales environments with sensitivity to current economic parameters and perceptions. Their economic challenge takes many forms, including retail entrepreneurs who are exploring a new product or market with limited resources, stores that seek the creative expression of inexpensive materials to suggest the economy and value of their product, and retail owners who desire the illusion of champagne space within a beer budget.

Entrepreneurs who are beginning to test their product seek to commission talented designers who understand the budget as a design challenge as opposed to a handicap. Oftentimes, the designer is challenged to produce an environment that is prototypical for future expansion of the product in other areas. Designers for such stores as Belle Rose and CLIX have created innovative spaces within limited resources for their client's first retail adventure.

History teaches us that retail product and design follow the economic path of our societies and the perception of current value. Such stores as St. Mark's Bookshop and Levi's Only utilize common off-the-shelf type materials such as plumbing hardware for shelf supports and rough grade 2 x 4 lumber in exposed conditions to emphasize the practical, economical and utilitarian aspects of their products. In a growing trend, designers of retail environments around the world have exposed customers to unique uses of everyday materials in a fashionable response to budget design.

Many retailers want the perception of "rich" space within a limited budget. This challenge has provided designers with the opportunity to push ordinary materials to do extraordinary things—sophisticated painting techniques suggesting elaborate surfaces and inexpensive woods, such as maple stained to resemble mahogany. Stores such as Mizani Uomo, Avant Garde, and Communicate have effectively combined many techniques to produce provocative spaces within limited resources.

Avant Garde
Women's Apparel/Accessories

Beverly Hills, California

An upscale line of European women's clothing for a fashion boutique in Beverly Hills challenged Kirkpatrick Associates Architects to integrate a suitably upscale environment with a minimal budget.

Avant Garde—meaning "vanguard of the arts, or at the forefront of a movement"—sought a sophisticated and comfortable environment for the display of its hand-picked clothing line. Using common materials in contrasting warm and cold finishes, the design attempted to fuse inexpensive and traditional materials in a contemporary setting.

The original space was gutted and the existing brick walls exposed. New walls of integrated color plaster were combined with rusted steel columns, hanging fixture supports, and sales platforms. Custom mahogany stained maple display furniture, standing mirrors, and fixed display cases with glass tops organize the circulation of the floor plan.

The 2,200 square foot store was completed in six weeks at a cost of $65 per square foot.

Owner/Company
NADIR & MIRELLE MANISH

Architect/Designer
KIRKPATRICK ASSOCIATES
ARCHITECTS, AIA

Design Team
GRANT KIRKPATRICK, RUSSELL
HATFIELD, ANDREW KAVAHARA

Contractor
HERB STEWART CONTRACTORS

Photographer
BREWSTER & BREWSTER

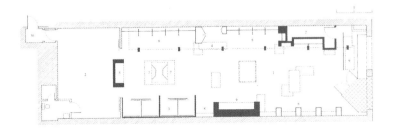

Mizani Uomo

Custom Men's Apparel

San Francisco, California

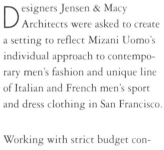

Owner/Company
ZAINO MIZANI

Architect/Designer
JENSEN & MACY ARCHITECTS

Lighting Designer
JENSEN & MACY ARCHITECTS

Furniture/Fixtures
JENSEN & MACY ARCHITECTS

Contractor
JAN PEARCE & BOB COLEMAN

Photographer
ALAN WEINTRAUB

Designers Jensen & Macy Architects were asked to create a setting to reflect Mizani Uomo's individual approach to contemporary men's fashion and unique line of Italian and French men's sport and dress clothing in San Francisco.

Working with strict budget controls, the architects used a combination of hardwood and brass—materials found in traditional haberdashery interiors—to highlight the merchandise and define the personal identity of Mizani Uomo.

The store's organization includes two distinct spaces. The first space is circular in shape and offers off-the-rack articles. The second is a rectangular room reserved for more exclusive merchandise, which includes garments tailored under Mizani Uomo's own label and custom-made suits. Unique combinations of simple materials and innovative attention are given to pragmatic retail store design issues. These include a custom display bay and lighting system composed entirely of hardwoods (maple and mahogany-stained cherry) and semi-precious metals (brass and bronze).

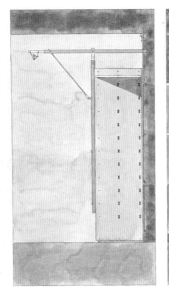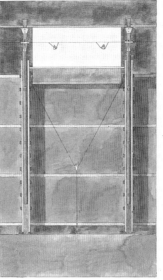

The heating, ventilation and cooling system breathes through a luminescent fabric ceiling, eliminating the need for air registers or ductwork which can distract the customer from the merchandise.

Completed in one month at approximately $60 per square foot, the solutions chosen transcend the limitations of space and budget to communicate the store's values and personal identity.

St. Mark's Bookshop
Books/Literature/Poems/Magazines

New York, New York

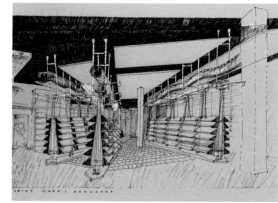

Challenged by a limited budget, an awkward space, and very little time, Zivkovic Associates Architects created an abstract and distinctive new space for St. Mark's Bookshop in downtown Manhattan.

To satisfy an alternative clientele and differentiate the image of the store from that of the established chain stores throughout the city, the imagery of the interior brings together some of the raw aesthetics associated with the East Village neighborhood. The radiating disposition of the central bookshelf units helps to reinforce this concept in addition to allowing visual surveillance of the sales area from the control desk. The control desk is conceived as the center of the store where the distribution of the utilities emanate. Air conditioning ducts undulate like a giant "slinky" across an open ceiling.

Owner/Company
ST. MARK'S BOOKSHOP
BOB CONTANT, TERRY MCCOY

Architect/Designer
ZIVKOVIC ASSOCIATES
ARCHITECTS P.C.

Project Design Team
DON ZIVKOVIC, BRIAN CONNOLLY

Project Assistants
DECLAN CULLEN, HOWARD DUFFY,
HUGH HIGGINS

Mechanical/Electrical Engineer
RANDALL POET (PROJECT ENGINEER),
MOTTOLA-POET ASSOCIATES

Lighting Designer
GARY GORDON, GARY GORDON
ARCHITECTURAL LIGHTING

Graphic Designer
WYNN DANN DESIGN (STORE LOGO)

Contractors
LJM CONSTRUCTION INC. (GENERAL
CONTRACTORS), M.O.S. ELECTRICAL
(POWER AND LIGHTING SYSTEMS)

Photographer
ASHLEY RANSON/RANSON BLACK
LIMITED

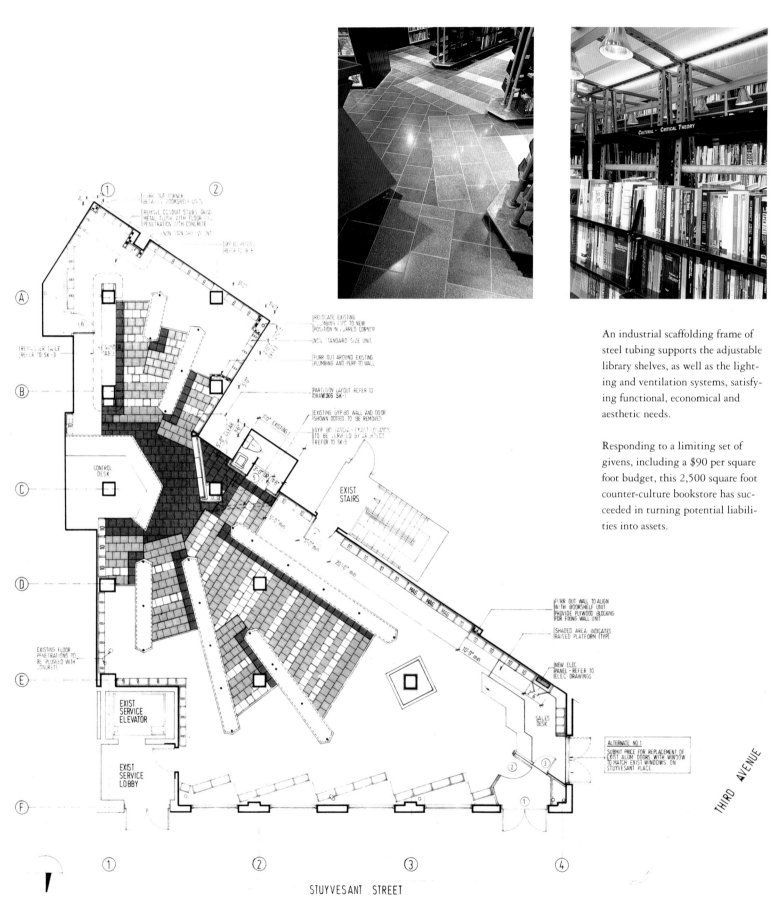

An industrial scaffolding frame of steel tubing supports the adjustable library shelves, as well as the lighting and ventilation systems, satisfying functional, economical and aesthetic needs.

Responding to a limiting set of givens, including a $90 per square foot budget, this 2,500 square foot counter-culture bookstore has succeeded in turning potential liabilities into assets.

THIRD AVENUE

STUYVESANT STREET

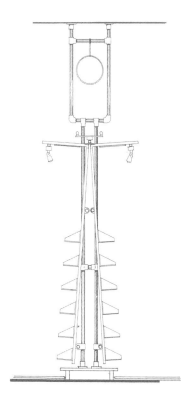

Otto Tootsi Plohound

Men's and Women's Shoes

New York, New York

With a theatrical combination of raw materials and industrial overtones, Walz Design Inc. has made shoes center stage in the new Otto Tootsi Plohound store on Fifth Avenue in Manhattan.

The designer was challenged both to keep an eye on the budget and to create a retail environment that would remain fresh for the length of the ten-year lease. The resulting design uses unusual materials chosen for their texture, color, and economy, to support the "fashion-forward" product lines of men's and women's shoes. Burlap and tar walls combine with stained chipboard and belted leather display tables, and solid ebonized oak shelving. Raw materials such as standing seam copper roofing used as wall finishes, slate flooring, and custom-designed industrial lighting fixtures were chosen for their form, function, and economy.

The 3,000 square foot store was constructed in three months at a cost of $100 per square foot.

Owner/Company
LARRY AND ANNETTE EVERSTON

Architect/Designer
WALZ DESIGN INC.

Graphic Designer
WALZ DESIGN INC.

Lighting Designer
WALZ DESIGN INC.

Contractor
SILVER RAIL CONSTRUCTION

Photographer
ANDREW GARN

Cornucopia

Flower Store

New York, New York

Wormser + Associates, Architects were given two weeks, a limited budget, and a charge to "shake things up" for the design of the Cornucopia floral boutique in New York.

The owner wanted to rattle the store's "stuffy old neighborhood" with something exciting, quick and inexpensive. Peter Wormser, AIA responded with a gentle play on the variety, color and whimsy of the merchandise itself. A quirky, shifting theme incorporating

Architect/Designer
WORMSER + ASSOCIATES, ARCHITECTS

Contractor
PAUL DEPRETER

Graphic Designer
MINA DOLBOWSKY

Photographer
© DAVID LUBARSKY

crooked steel windows and colorfully stained plywood panels permeates the space. Other materials include sandblasted glass, custom steel and concrete furniture, and maple plywood.

The 600 square foot store was closed for two weeks to complete construction. The $50,000 cost included the architect designed sconces fabricated from garden tool forks and trowels.

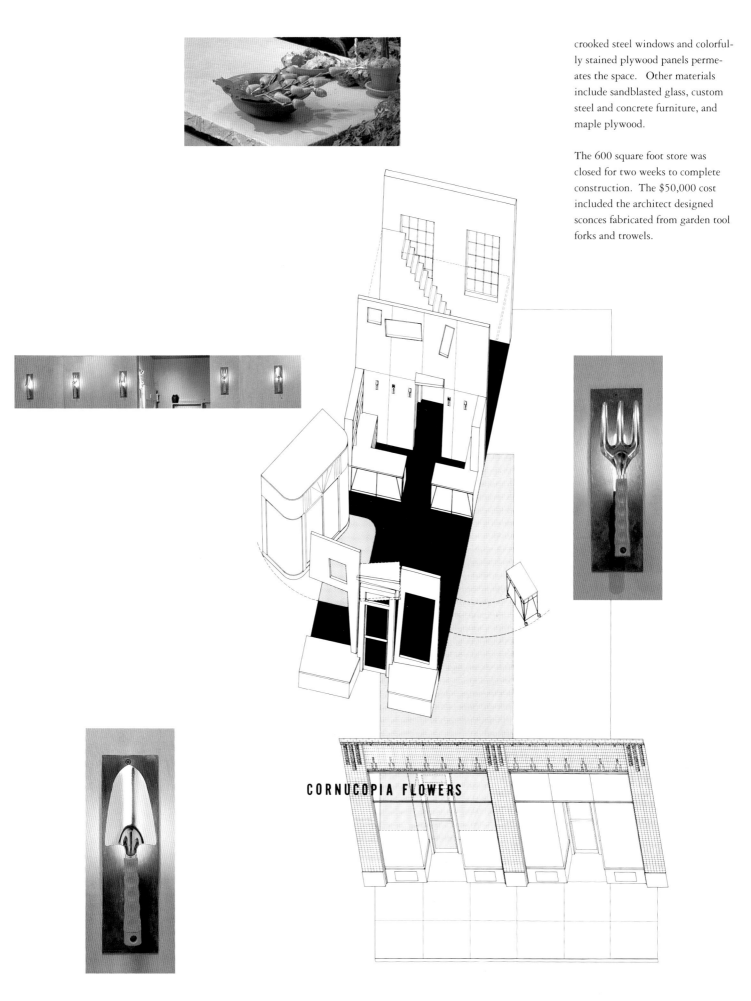

CORNUCOPIA FLOWERS

pH Neutro
Perfume

Florence, Italy

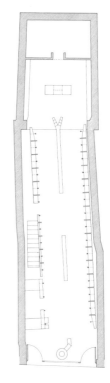

The need to display a vast quantity of small items combined with an extremely limited construction budget led Jensen & Macy Architects to design the simple, rigorous shelving system for this perfume boutique.

Long narrow display counters snake through this syncopated volume. These solid, simple structures stand in contrast to the light, lattice-like structure of the perimeter. The central counter is a completely closed tall and narrow box mounted to the floor. The head of this cabinet rests in the storefront window and consists of three cantilevered disks. The tail, at the back of the store, is a forked projection consisting of open bins for the display of small items. Together, they give a beginning and end to the composition of the store which is dominated by the continuous field of shelving.

The display system allows the colorfully painted existing walls to read through as a backdrop. A costly and time-consuming confrontation was avoided by detaching the shelving system from the irregular walls. The wood is a thin clear-sealed plywood with exposed edges. The plywood piece, placed perpendicular to the shelf and back panel for stability, has a slightly curved front edge. This piece varies in its extension from shelf to shelf and forms a subtle arc when viewed from the side. Clear-sealed metal brackets and feet support beechwood poles, which in turn carry the shelves.

Built in two months at a cost of less than $40 per square foot, the simple, utilitarian components produce an intriguing rhythm and texture in the 800 square foot space.

Owner/Company
PH NEUTRO

Architect/Designer
JENSEN & MACY ARCHITECTS

Graphic Designer
MARINA TACCHI

Lighting Designer
JENSEN & MACY ARCHITECTS

Contractor
YURI BRASCHI

Photographer
PABLO BALARIN

Dobson Telephone Company, Inc.

Telephone Systems

Oklahoma City, Oklahoma

Educating the customer became the design focus for the new retail space designed by Elliott + Associates Architects for Dobson Telephone Company in Oklahoma City.

In an effort to inform the customer of the advantages of the cellular telephone, the architects developed a plan to introduce a historical perspective about communication in conjunction with the display of the latest cellular communications equipment. A generous space allowed several design elements to organize the store. The entry gallery illustrates the history of telephone communications with display niches highlighting examples of historically significant telephone instruments. A 24 foot long stainless steel display sculpture for new products symbolizes precision, high technology, and flexibility.

Owner/Company
DOBSON TELEPHONE COMPANY, INC.

Architect/Designer
ELLIOTT + ASSOCIATES ARCHITECTS

Interior Designer
ELLIOTT + ASSOCIATES ARCHITECTS

Graphic Designer
RAND ELLIOTT, AIA

Lighting Designer
RAND ELLIOTT, AIA

Contractor
CLYDE RIGGS CONSTRUCTION

Photographer
BOB SHIMER, HEDRICH BLESSING,
CHICAGO, ILLINOIS

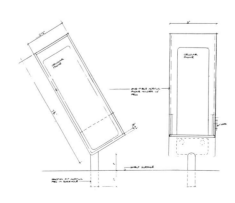

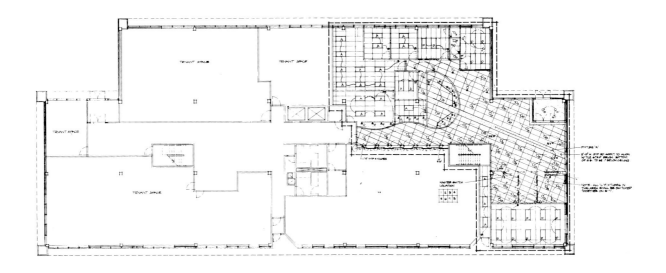

The store attempts to override several limitations by infusing a kinetic imagery to the space that alludes to the high-tech nature of the product through a "line of communication." The display sculpture, linear floor tile, and overhead lighting system create a horizontal dynamic to counteract an 8 foot ceiling height. Odd configurations are overcome with an undulating corrugated fiberglass wall that encloses offices and inventory areas and becomes a "visual energy source." A Spartan use of bold primary colors highlights the store's relatively few number of small products.

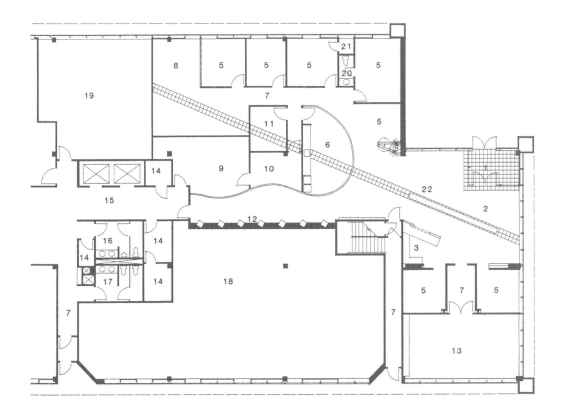

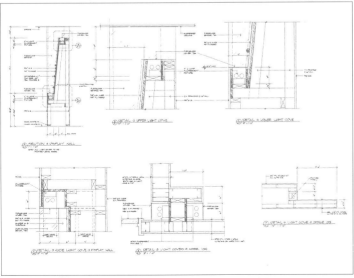

Salon Secrets

Haircare Products

Surrey, England

Architect/Designer
FITCH

Project Team
MARTYN BEST, STUART NAYSMITH,
STEWART HUNTER, SIMON NEALE,
LEE SMITH

Photographer
JOHN LINDEN

As a new prototype and the first store of its kind in Europe, Salon Secrets, by Fitch, combines styling, consultation and retail of professional haircare products and accessories.

The design entices the customer to discover the advantages of product and service in a one-stop environment. Haircare products and professional accessories are displayed in the entry area for higher retail sales. The treatment area, with four hair and two nail stations, is in the middle of the store. Customers who have a haircut, styling or manicure can be guided to buy one of the products the stylist has used. A free consultation from the professional styling staff encourages customers to buy the best products for their particular requirements.

A bold palette, lifestyle graphics and large "text" panels are used throughout the store to identify and explain the products and services and create a welcoming mood.

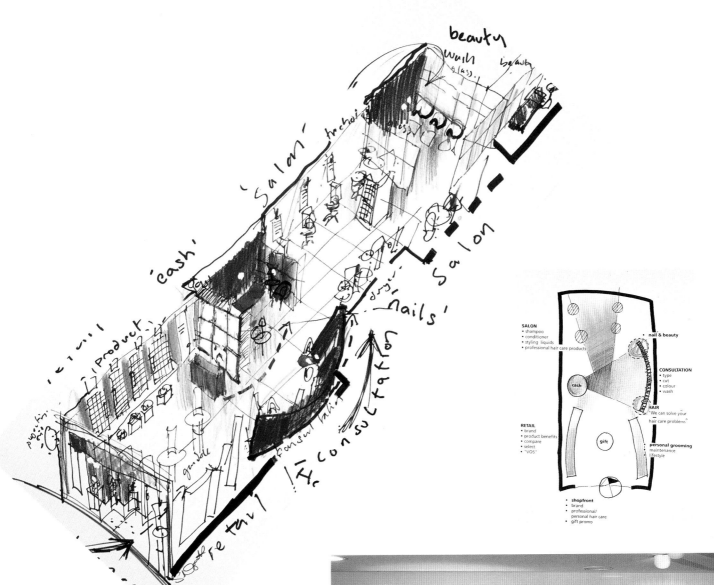

SALON
• shampoo
• conditioner
• styling liquids
• professional hair care products

nail & beauty

CONSULTATION
• type
• cut
• colour
• wash

cash

HAIR
"We can solve your
hair care problems"

RETAIL
• brand
• product benefits
• compare
• select
• "VOS"

gift

personal grooming
maintenance
lifestyle

• shopfront
• brand
• professional/
  personal hair care
• gift promo

Communicate

Telephone Systems

Chicago, Illinois

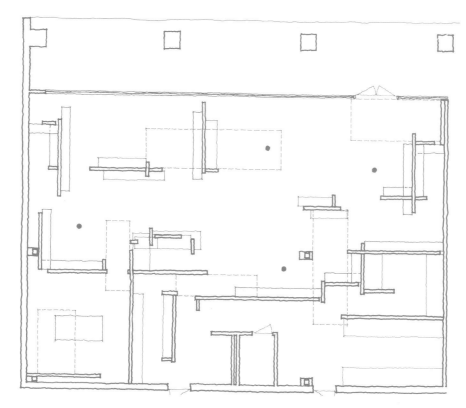

With a minimal budget and tight time schedule, Florian • Wierzbowski was challenged to create a museum-like setting for the sales and demonstration of the latest telephone systems for Communicate.

A planar series of white walls delineates a series of spaces and focuses the customer's attention on the product demonstration areas. Freestanding concrete pedestals mark the various sales areas and refer to the corporate logo. Horizontal display surfaces are sheathed in colored formica with under-counter lighting to create the illusion of intersecting planes floating in the space. The ceiling is left exposed to reinforce the high-tech exhibit of merchandise. Spot lighting of the merchandise consists of par lamps in porcelain sockets that drop from the exposed ceiling.

Various ancillary facilities include office space for the owners and sales staff as well as storage and expediting areas. A conference area permits demonstrations of custom systems designed for particular clients.

Owner/Company
MARC ZIONTS, IAN AARON

Architect/Designer
FLORIAN • WIERZBOWSKI
ARCHITECTURE, P.C.

Partners
PAUL FLORIAN
STEPHEN WIERZBOWSKI
WILLIAM WORN (PROJECT ARCHITECT)
TED THEODORE
JEFF HENRIKSEN

Graphic Designer
MICHAEL GLASS, MICHAEL GLASS
DESIGN

Lighting Designer
FLORIAN WIERZBOWSKI
ARCHITECTURE, P.C.

Contractor
BARRY GLASSER

Photographer
BARBARA KARANT/KARANT &
ASSOCIATES

Belle Rose

Flowers

Chicago, Illinois

Tainer Associates, Ltd. created a three-dimensional grid of metal trusses somewhat like a giant Erector Set to economically organize the new Belle Rose flagship retail store for an Ecuadorian rose grower.

Located in the two-story lobby of a downtown high-rise, the 1,500 square foot space called for a flexible and budget conscious design. Using metal trusses, the designers developed adjustable shelving for flower displays, storage cabinets, and wrap stations. An overhead grid of trusses stabilizes the entire freestanding system and provides support for lighting, signage and other features. This system alludes to an outdoor trellis and provides a human scale to the relatively tall space. It also takes advantage of the "fishbowl" situation created by the existing perimeter glass for maximum product visibility.

Owner/Company
BELLE ROSE

Architect/Designer
TAINER ASSOCIATES, LTD.

Contractor
CHICAGO INTERIOR
CONSTRUCTION CORP.

Project Team
DARIO TAINER AIA (PRINCIPAL)
ANDREW GROEGER
ADRIENNE BRODIN
CARLA SURMA
KURT WILLIAMS
CLARK ELLITHORPE (MURALS)

Graphic Designer
TAINER ASSOCIATES, LTD.

Lighting Designer
TAINER ASSOCIATES, LTD.

Photographer
FRANCOIS ROBERT

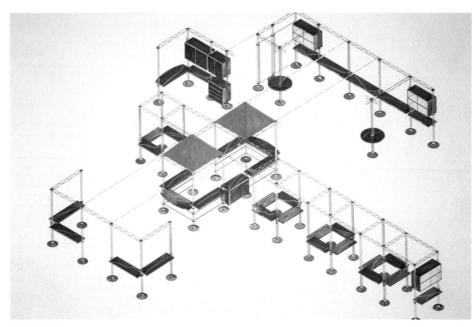

Color for the space is provided by the merchandise, as the store carries at least 16 different types of roses. Therefore, all fixturing was specified black. Two red canvas canopies designate the counter area which itself is situated on a smooth field of green tile. A pre-Columbian mural on the only solid wall in the space completes the synthesis of the products' origins and the store's contemporary sales venue.

A/X Armani Exchange

Apparel

New York, New York

Owner/Company
GIORGIO ARMANI CORPORATION

Architect/Designer
NAOMI LEFF + ASSOCIATES

With an artful juxtaposition of the elemental and the refined, Naomi Leff + Associates, in conjunction with Giorgio Armani, has created a relaxed sales context for the new A/X Armani Exchange store in the SoHo area of New York.

As the exclusive home of the Armani Jeans Collection, the free-standing 3,500 square foot building simultaneously evokes the imagery of an expansive military building and a sophisticated European bistro. This concept reflects the designer's personal preferences in color, style and sense of space, and develops a complementary textural and tonal composition for the merchandise, which includes denim and cotton.

Mr. Armani's own weekend house on Pantelleria, an island off the coast of Sicily, is part of the inspiration for this unique store. The rusted patina of natural volcanic rock, sandy beaches and sun-bleached wood is reflected in the store's finishes—grey-bleached wood counters and weathered wood floors. The designers' use of "poor" or basic materials in refined conditions was inspired by the work of

Parisian designer Pierre Chareau whom Mr. Armani has long admired. The design also borrows from Chareau's sense of wide open space and warm light. Italian street lights with glass globes underscore the simple but refined approach to every detail.

Accessibility was Mr. Armani's foremost detail when conceiving the store. From the angled, gridded tables to the shelving and fixtures, everything was designed for quick access and self-service.

Regional Transportation Authority Retail
Public Transportation Regulatory Agency Retail

Chicago, Illinois

STEVE HALL, HEDRICH-BLESSING

Chicago's Regional Transportation Authority (RTA) hired The Environments Group, Inc. and 555 DFM to create a new retail facility to distribute information, literature, and passes to commuters. By projecting the agency's spirit of transportation and accommodation, the design invites the commuter into the information center.

Owner/Company
REGIONAL TRANSPORTATION
AUTHORITY (RTA)

Architect/Designer
THE ENVIRONMENTS GROUP, INC.

Graphic Designer/Lighting Designer
CAROL PENFOLD (PROJECT MANAGER)

Design/Fabricator of Metal Objects
555 DESIGN FABRICATION
MANAGEMENT (555 DFM)

Contractor
CONTINENTAL INTERIORS

Photographers
PETER WILLIAMSON/SUE KEZOH
(555 DFM)
STEVE HALL (HEDRICH-BLESSING)

STEVE HALL, HEDRICH-BLESSING

STEVE HALL, HEDRICH-BLESSING

Located in the heart of the city's business center at the pedestrian level directly adjacent to Chicago's elevated railway, the storefront intrigues passersby with a series of triangular pylons featuring over-sized cut-outs of stainless steel human figures running to catch a train or bus. These figures function as a sign, a display fixture for maps, and the architectonic element of the space. The repetition of these freeze-framed elements depicted in a dynamic posture reinforces the spirit of movement.

The machinery and infrastructure of railway transportation influenced the materials. Stainless and cold rolled steel, terrazzo flooring, layered glass, etched aluminum, and perforated metal panels express the rationalism and utilitarianism prevalent in the RTA facility.

The design is born out of a fundamental understanding of the agency's utilitarian purpose and fiscal constraints. At a budget of $40 per square foot, the result reflects the agency's spirit of transportation and responsibility to the urban community.

Levi's Only

Casual Apparel

Ontario, Canada

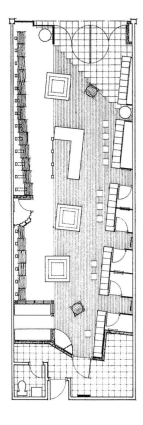

Echoing the frontier heritage of Levi Strauss & Co., the new Levi's Only store fabricated by The International Design Group picks up on the utilitarian nature of the Levi product within the context of today's consumer appeal.

The retailer's goal of a fun, universally appealing store was carried one step further with environmentally sensitive materials and display systems used to organize the 1,400 square foot space. Distinct display areas include the "Hanging Galley," made up of a series of construction-grade 2" x 4" uprights and beams; the "Great Wall of Jeans," composed of five bin units that form a wall at an angle from the front to the back of the store; and the "Little House of Alterations," with its board-and-batten style.

Built in eight weeks at a cost of $70 per foot, the end product of the designers' imaginative and cost-effective use of common materials successfully retails a tried and true product in today's marketplace.

Owner/Company
KEITH KOVAR

Architect/Designer
THE INTERNATIONAL DESIGN GROUP

Graphic Designer
RUSS WARREN

Lighting Designer
E.A. REA

Contractor
FLOOT CONSTRUCTION DESIGN

Photographer
MASAO ABE PHOTOGRAPHY

Roche Bobois
Classic Contemporary Furniture

Boston, Massachusetts

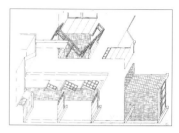

A careful analysis of product, space and budget allowed Bergmeyer Associates to infuse the Roche Bobois Boston furniture store with a creative mix of materials within an extremely limited budget.

The international retailer of contemporary furniture wanted their showroom to maximize flexibility and convey a sense of openness to allow the shopper to focus on individual furniture settings. With $20 per square foot and 10,000 square feet to work with, the designers incorporated a series of background elements that would sustain the needed flexibility and bring attention to the merchandise. Intermediate height panels define room settings and help to control vistas throughout the space. The panels form the framework for fabric coverings which act as backdrops for the furniture settings.

Materials were chosen as a response to the store's Boston context: the blues and greens in the ceramic tile recall Boston's waterfront; marble and sandstone honor the masonry traditions of the city's North End.

Owner/Company
SKIP AND GINA FREEMAN

Architect/Designer
BERGMEYER ASSOCIATES

Principal-in-Charge
JOSEPH P. NEVIN, JR.

Project Architect
MICHAEL R. DAVIS, AIA

Interior Designers
MICHAEL R. DAVIS, AIA
GINA FREEMAN

Faux Finishes
MATTHEW HOYDIC

Millworker
COMMERCIAL CASEWORK CO.

Lighting Designer
RIPMAN LIGHTING CONSULTANTS

Contractor
PORTER CONSTRUCTION

Photographer
LUCY CHEN

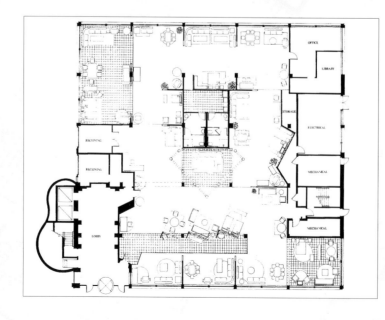

CLIX

Commercial Photography

Westminster, California

Owner/Company
CLIX

Architect/Designer
ROCKEFELLER/HRICAK ARCHITECTS

Partners
DARRELL ROCKEFELLER, AIA
MICHAEL HRICAK, AIA

Project Designer
ANDREA BELLON

Structural Engineer
STEVEN W. MEZEY & ASSOCIATES

Electrical Engineer
MOSES & ASSOCIATES

Lighting Design
ROCKEFELLER/HRICAK ARCHITECTS

Millwork
FRANK BARBER FINE CABINETRY

Metal Fabrication & Custom Light Fixture
R. SCHER & ASSOCIATES

Graphic Design Consultant
FREEMAN KARTEN

Sign Fabricator
PETER CARLSON ENTERPRISES

Contractor
HILTON CONSTRUCTION CO.

Photographer
DAVID GLOMB

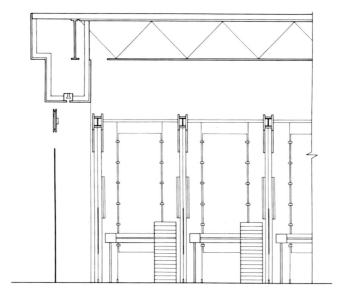

SECTION EAST-WEST LOOKING SOUTH

Using fashion as the ultimate metaphor for design, Rockefeller/Hricak Architects have given a makeover to a retail concept based on a variation of commercial portrait photography.

Clix is a fashion photography studio where the customer is transformed with a complete makeover, then photographed in a "model for a day" session. Transformation therefore, was central to the architects' design. Ordinary materials are utilized in unusual ways serving both a functional and aesthetic value. Plywood frames and structures create a framework for various secondary design elements including mirrors, glass privacy screens and photo murals.

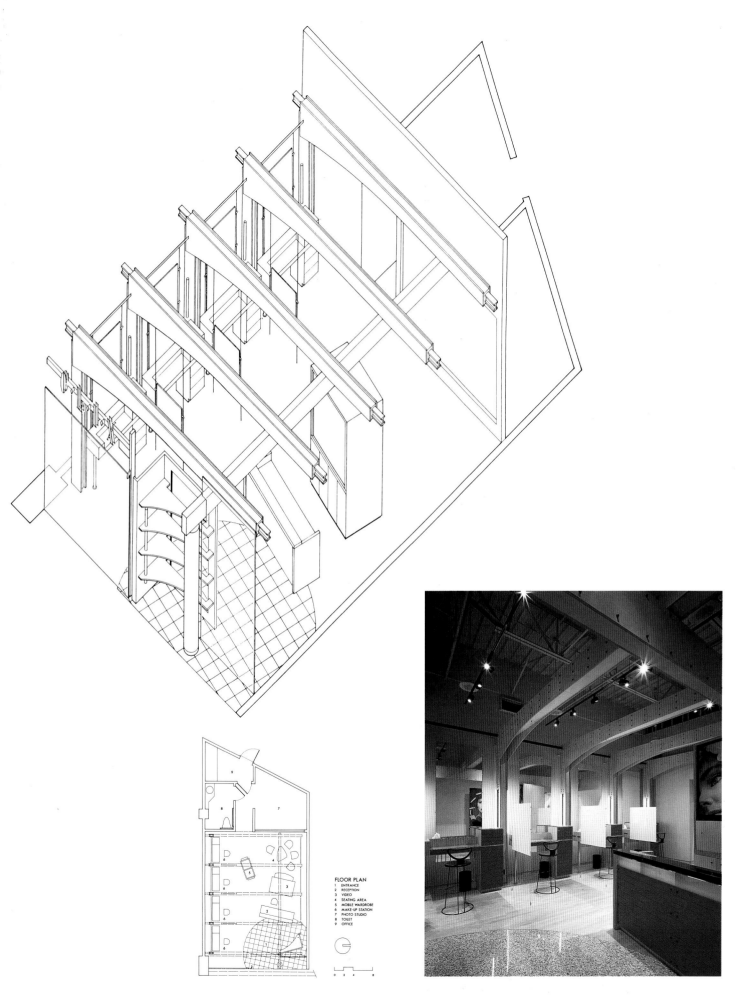

FLOOR PLAN
1 ENTRANCE
2 RECEPTION
3 VIDEO
4 SEATING AREA
5 MOBILE WARDROBE
6 MAKE-UP STATION
7 PHOTO STUDIO
8 TOILET
9 OFFICE

0 2 4 8

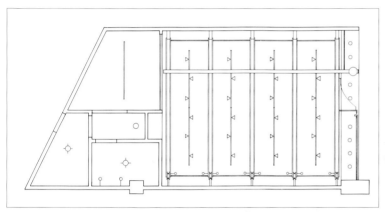

As a possible prototype for future locations, the 920 square foot studio has flexibility. The number of make-up station units can be expanded or reduced according to the various configurations and sizes of other spaces.

Unconventional Venues

As specific retail markets expand or contract and competition becomes more intense, many retailers look for unconventional ways to attract potential customers and retain the loyalty of their existing customer base. Although the "every square foot counts" adage still reigns, some stores are recognizing a need to be different and have successfully pushed beyond the conventional shopping experience. These unconventional venues include stores which have integrated a special feature or venue within the space, stores that have combined retail sales and showroom uses, and stores which have been conceived to promote newly developed products.

Retail history has taught that the more time a customer spends in a store, the more likely he or she is to make a purchase. Following this logic, many new stores and boutiques such as Emporio Armani, Casakit Equippe, and Felissimo have integrated restaurants, bars, and coffee/tea rooms within their retail venues. Other stores such as the World Foot Locker with its chain-link fenced half-court basketball arena, have created dynamic focal points for their sales areas that may attract potential customers' attention or creatively display new merchandise.

Showrooms, typically flexible spaces for the wholesale display of fashion merchandise, have become integral for the designers of high-end fashions. Many retailers have found creative means to combine their showrooms with retail sales to take advantage of the inherent customer crossover. The many flexible and innovative spaces that result include the Urban Outfitters Wholesale Showroom, Joseph Abboud, and Sara Sturgeon.

Entrepreneurial spirit, technology, and foreign influences provide ample opportunity for retailers to develop new products or merchandise for the consumer market. The success of a new product relies on the creation of the complete image for the merchandise to arouse interest in a crowded marketplace. Christopher Hansen Ltd and Giles & Lewis exemplify unconventional retail venues that blaze new trails of design for their embryonic markets.

Christopher Hansen Ltd

Audio/Video Showroom

Beverly Hills, California

With a healthy respect for the historical nature of the original building, and an understanding of the flexible requirements for the new retail venue, Kirkpatrick Associates Architects provided a synthesized environment for the first location of the Christopher Hansen Ltd Audio/Video Showroom.

The existing 5,400 square foot Art Deco building was structurally upgraded and restored to its original circa 1940s form. The new façade uses a simple palette of materials that recalls the similar design and functional qualities of the merchandise inside. Birch wood display arches, black granite banding and the juxtaposition of clear and diffused glass complete the exterior.

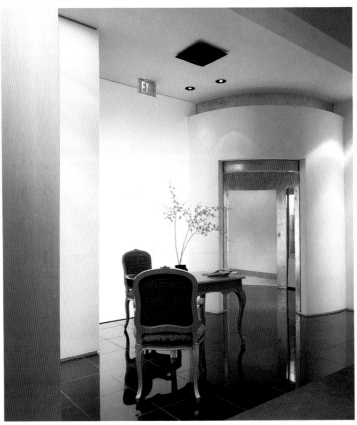

Owner/Company
CHRISTOPHER HANSEN LTD

Architect/Designer
KIRKPATRICK ASSOCIATES
ARCHITECTS, AIA

Design Team
GRANT KIRKPATRICK, STEVE
STRAUGHAN, RUSSELL HATFIELD,
RACHEL DOUGAN, CINDY UTTERBACK

Lighting Designer
GRENALD ASSOCIATES, LTD.
ALLENA APPIA

Contractor
TOTAL DEVELOPMENT

Photographer
BREWSTER & BREWSTER

The interior program required four acoustically engineered sound rooms for the display and operation of specialty audio merchandise. A THX Dolby video theater, a gallery hall for a variety of events, a video display room, conference room, and support spaces were also constructed. The entrance leads into the main gallery with sound rooms and subordinate spaces on each side. Beyond, an intimate rotunda acts as a transition space between the gallery and video and sound chambers where the ultra-esoteric equipment is displayed and operated.

The owner wanted the area where merchandise is used to relay a sense of the comfort of home. The colors, materials, and contrasting period furnishings create this mood and exhibit the flexibility of the merchandise for many environments. Extensive use of clear and diffused laminated glass provides light transmittance throughout, and privacy and sound attenuation from the busy retail street.

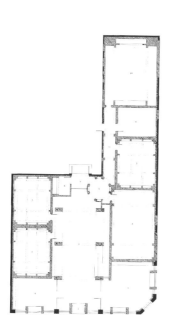

Emporio Armani
Apparel

San Francisco, California

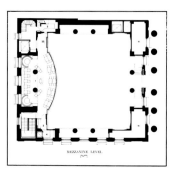

For Thane Roberts Architects, the conversion of a bank building into a retail store for the new Emporio Armani in San Francisco was as much an exercise in de-emphasizing imagery as it was in creating it.

The 12,000 square foot store is focused on the ground level where the majority of fashion merchandise is displayed. The beaux-arts classicism of the plan produces a powerful symmetry that rises 60 feet and terminates in a skylight cupola at the top of the dome. The mezzanine level, which was increased more than two-fold, projects into the main space and houses the dining area for the new restaurant. An additional sales area, service functions, and the kitchen are located in the basement. Upper levels are used exclusively for storage.

Owner/Company
GIORGIO ARMANI CORPORATION

Architect/Designer
THANE ROBERTS

Project Architect
AMINE ATLASCHI

Field Architect
JON ALFF

Interior Furnishings
GIANCARLO ORTELLI
GEERT DE TURCK

Correspondent Architect
FREEBAIRN-SMITH

Coordinating Architect
JANET CRANE

Lighting Consultant
ARCHITECTURAL LIGHTING DESIGN

Mechanical Engineer
AJMANI AND ASSOCIATES

Electrical Engineer
ZEIGER ENGINEERS, INC.

Contractor
DINWIDDIE CONSTRUCTION

Photographer
GIORGIO ARMANI CORPORATION

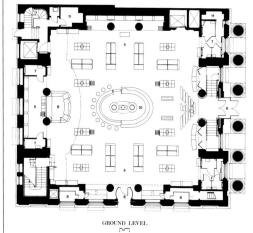

GROUND LEVEL

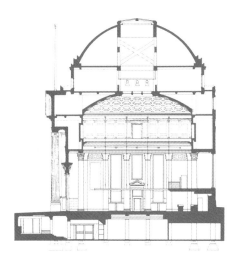

The retail store required a more approachable and intimate environment, and in order to impart the practical aspects of retail sales, portions of the new design depart from the historical character of the original building. Metal glass screens, a stainless steel balcony handrail, steel stairs and a tensile floating lighting system help to scale the space to human dimensions. Tall cabinet fixtures designed by the owner's Italian architect were configured for the main floor for usable display surfaces that the original marble surfaces and columns could not provide.

The central bar was designed as the focal point of the new boutique. Modeled after the boutique's European counterpart, this element brings focus and activity to the center of the store. A projecting balcony overlooks the bar and boutique and provides dining for 50 guests. Serviced by a dumbwaiter from the kitchen below, the dining mezzanine is encased by linen curtains and shares the dark mahogany details of the bar in the main sales area.

Urban Outfitters Wholesale

Apparel

New York, New York

Owner/Company
URBAN OUTFITTERS

President
RICHARD HAYNE

Creative Director
SUE OTTO

Architect/Designer
POMPEI A.D.

Design Principal
RON POMPEI

Custom Fixture Designer
POMPEI A.D., NEW YORK CITY

Fixture Fabricator
CHANDLER AND PATON

Graphic Designer
URBAN OUTFITTERS

Custom Finishes
OTTO INDUSTRIES,
CUTWATER BLUE, INC.

Contractor
J.I. MASTER BUILDERS, INC.

Photographer
© TOM CRANE

Pompei A.D., the architectural firm responsible for the design of the Urban Outfitters stores, integrated the signature aesthetics and imagery of the company for the design of their new showroom in a 6,000 square foot space in New York City's garment district.

Without the need to garner every square foot for merchandise, the project team was able to emphasize the materials, finishes and sculptural aspects of the stores the showroom represents. Exposed brick, concrete, steel, and distressed finishes, as well as yellow wainscoting and galvanized metal take the experimental imagery of the store one step further.

The removal of existing dropped ceilings created a 12 foot high space. Four showrooms were built along the west window wall, providing maximum light for apparel display. Partial walls separate showrooms and a semi-private common workspace, allowing natural light to filter through. A gallery of offices was built closer to the building's core. A reception area with tables and chairs, telephones, and a cappuccino bar provides buyers with what Ron Pompei calls "a calm in the middle of the hurricane of market week." A gallery wall displays current fashions sketched on corrugated cardboard and stained plywood sculptures—now a signature of Urban stores.

Joseph Abboud
Apparel

New York, New York

An ongoing collaboration between the owner and designers, Bentley LaRosa Salasky, has allowed the new Joseph Abboud showroom to continue the evolution of the integration of the store design with the identity of the clothing line.

The 7,000 square foot New York showroom contains offices and interspersed showroom areas for the display of the various clothing lines. A sweeping display wall delineates the menswear showroom and terminates with a circular seating nook.

Owner/Company
J. A. APPAREL CORP.

Architect/Designer
BENTLEY LAROSA SALASKY,
ARCHITECTS & DECORATORS

Contractor
SHAWMUT DESIGN AND
CONSTRUCTION

Photographer
PAUL WARCHOL

The designers responded to the clothing's tactile sensibilities—subtle colors, layered textures and natural materials—with a palette of materials, colors and surfaces. Used extensively around doors and mirrors, carved solid cherry surrounds are scalloped to emphasize rich detail. Additional detail is apparent in the various finishes which include walnut, matte black lacquer, burlap, and steel. Custom details include wall sconces of cowhide simulated with fiberglass.

The Abboud diamond logo is used
extensively in various materials and
surfaces such as the Kilim carpets,
the herringbone parquet flooring
and the leather wrapped reception
desk with a diamond layout of
brass studs.

Custom-designed round tables of
cherry and Pakistani onyx are set
up for flexible groupings and
paired with rectangular desks that
accommodate larger buying groups.

Oasis
Perfume

Oakville, Ontario, Canada

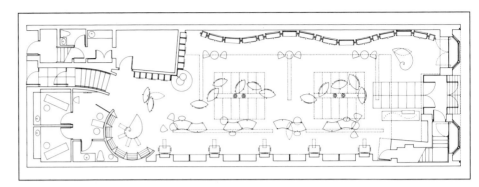

Traditionally, parfumerie and fragrance shops have been confined to counters in department stores or small boutiques, but Oasis in Ontario, designed by Kuwabara Payne McKenna Blumberg Architects, offers an innovative and flexible alternative for the sampling and purchase of fragrances, cosmetics, and accessories for men and women.

The designers were given a luxurious 3,000 square feet and instructions to create an atmosphere that would encourage customers to touch, sense, and explore the merchandise. Sensuous curvilinear sample tables float within a linear sales area defined by rigorously ordered wall display units. Areas of more intimate focus combine with the generous amount of circulation in the main area to suggest movement and informality in a unified spatial concept.

Owner/Company
OASIS PARFUMERIE INC.

Architect/Designer
KUWABARA PAYNE MCKENNA
BLUMBERG ARCHITECTS

Project Team
BRUCE KUWABARA, SHIRLEY
BLUMBERG, KAREN PETRACHENKO,
TODD MACYK, DAVID JESSON

Lighting Designer
KUWABARA PAYNE MCKENNA
BLUMBERG ARCHITECTS

Contractor
MILLWORKS CUSTOM
FABRICATORS INC.

Photographer
STEVEN EVANS

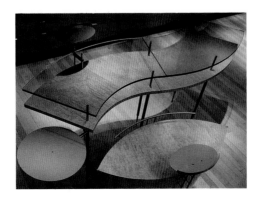

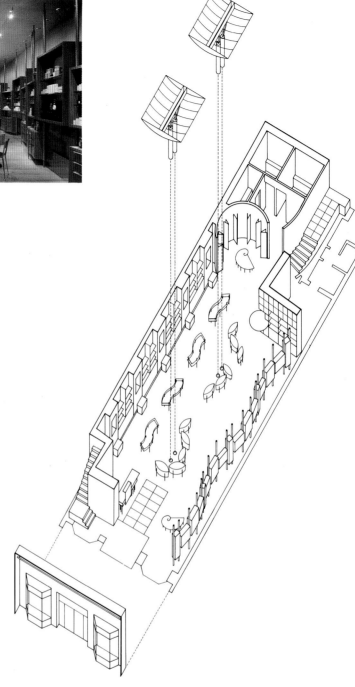

Natural materials are used throughout the store including maple hardwood flooring, Piasentina granite floor slabs, and custom-designed display units crafted of European beech and maple veneers.

Felissimo

Specialty Apparel/Home Furnishings

New York, New York

An abandoned six-story residential building in downtown Manhattan provided Clodagh Design International with a mixed bag of parameters to create a mini department store, complete with four floors of retail and conference areas, and a tearoom.

The year-long refurbishment of this 12,000 square foot turn-of-the-century building applied practical issues within a very unorthodox layout. In addition to the store's variety of merchandise, issues such as handicap accessibility, mechanical systems, and environmental concerns were carefully synthesized into a surreal context. The designer sought to relate all the senses by utilizing sensuous finishes, organic fixtures, and rich natural colors. Even the exterior of the building, originally grey, was stained a lively ochre to look sunny on the greyest day.

Owner/Company
FELISSIMO UNIVERSAL CORPORATION

Architect/Designer
CLODAGH DESIGN INTERNATIONAL

Graphic Design
STUDIO N

Lighting Design
CLODAGH DESIGN INTERNATIONAL

Contractor
KAJIMA INTERNATIONAL

Photographer
DANIEL AUBRY

The owner and designer were firmly united in their desire to create an inviting town house atmosphere to celebrate the work and energy of a group of applied artists. The energy created by every finish and detail encourages the shopper to explore the merchandise comfortably before stopping on the fourth floor for a refreshing tea.

The air is scented with stimulating essential oils. A sparkling rivulet of water flows over stacked glass at the information desk. Surfaces are tactile and each store fixture is an individual art piece which enhances rather than overpowers the merchandise.

Environmental concerns were addressed in many aspects of the design. Nonthreatened woods were used in the fabrication of fixtures and cabinetry. The natural patinas of bronze and copper reduced the use of sealers. Rich, evocative surfaces were created with nontoxic finishes on walls, floors and store fixtures. Colors were chosen from a sensuous natural palette—ochre, parchment, copper, amber, oxidized green, terra cotta and Pompeiian red.

Sara Sturgeon

Apparel

Los Angeles, California

The dichotomy of a retail store and showroom occupying the same reformed warehouse space allowed designer Rafi Balouzian to develop a thematic approach to separate the two functions.

The design was conceived as a modern interpretation of a medieval fortress. Separation of showroom from sales floor was whimsically achieved by a series of program elements including maple veneer walls fortified with sheet metal-wrapped support columns and dressing room "tents" hung from the ceiling. A "bridge" connects the sales area to the showroom, warehouse, and office spaces. Constructed of a bent steel plate and exposed timber, the bridge was conceived as a mental transition to create interest for the everyday circulation of the employees and customers. The owner conceives the separation of the spaces as a protection of her future designs from people other than the buyers.

Flexibility for future expansion of the retail area without construction and use of the showroom for shipping purposes during peak times was required. All of the custom-designed furniture and fixtures were created to reinforce the medieval theme and are left in their natural colors. The project was completed in 14 weeks at a cost of less than $40 per square foot.

Owner/Company
SARA STURGEON

Architect/Designer
RAFI BALOUZIAN

Contractor
SHABCON

Photographer
© 1994 TOM BONNER

Casakit Equippe
Furniture

Scarsdale, New York

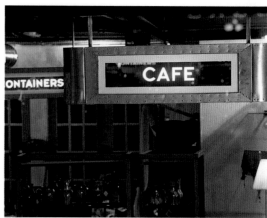

Owner/Company
CASAKIT EQUIPPE

Architect/Designer
CLODAGH DESIGN INTERNATIONAL

Designer
CLODAGH

Architect
ROBERT PIERPONT

Project Director
DAVID HOWELL

Graphic Designer
GRAFX

Lighting Designer
CLODAGH DESIGN INTERNATIONAL

Specialist Lighting Signs
DAVID ROSENCRANZ

Contractor
ANTHONY PIAZZA

Photographer
DANIEL AUBRY

Casakit, an Italian kitchen manufacturer, commissioned Clodagh Design International to develop a new concept for the "boutique" display and sales of a highly diverse product line.

The rusticated entry is fashioned from recycled lumber, copper sheathing, and custom hardware signifying the disparate combination of decorative accessories, furniture, and kitchen and bath accessories for sale within. Merchandise,

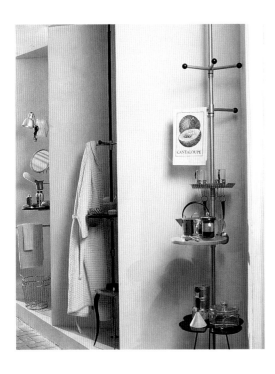

including seven types of model kitchens, is divided into "shops," identified by hanging signs that denote the products within. Customers move to different sales areas via passages designed as "streets." Custom lighting fixtures that mimic streetlights illuminate the pathways and reinforce the concept.

The combination of the street of shops concept and rusticated material palette of the 5,000 square foot space provides a cohesive environment for a varied product line.

Ocella

Eyewear

Belfast, Ireland

Within an existing Victorian church in downtown Belfast, Fitch has created a new store for the sale of luxury-brand eyewear and ophthalmic services called Ocella.

Pitched to the high end of the market, the store concept is based around quality of service, product and environment—an idiom that permeates every level of the design from the layout to the fixtures, materials, custom lighting, and furniture. A mix of name-brand products is offered within three levels of display allowing flexibility of arrangement and control over customer interaction. This involves tabletop display, wall units, and stand-alone showcases for the top-of-the-line eyewear.

Screened from the main store, the rear of the ground floor is an informal waiting area that doubles as the lens treatment space. Upstairs is a fully enclosed consulting room where the furnishings and materials continue the theme of the store.

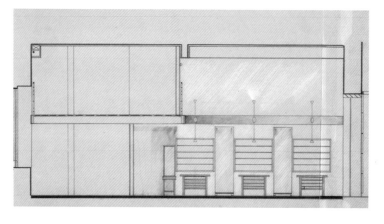

Owners
HILARY WILSON AND RODNEY LECKIE

Architect/Designer
FITCH

Metal Fixtures and Fittings
BOB BOOTH, EX RON ARAD

Photographer
CHRISTOPHER HILL

The minimal tenor of the space comes from a visual dialogue between old and new. This is suggested in the product, which mixes contemporary and traditional themes, and the site, a modern development within an older building. An eclectic mix of period pieces sits within the simple shell bounded by mutual planes of color. A painted timber floor with a geometric motif, by Thomas Lane, combines with this shell to restore order and set up a datum throughout the space.

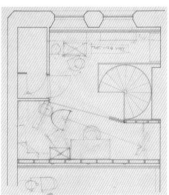

Giles & Lewis

High-Profile Design Products

New York, New York

Using a strong architectural order and minimal building intervention within an unorthodox existing structure, Mojo•Stumer Architects created an environment to highlight the adventurous nature of Giles & Lewis's high-profile merchandise.

A turn-of-the-century brick and concrete structure, the building presented many design challenges including minimal store frontage, an inflexible structural layout and years of unrecorded additions. These challenges, and the desire to exploit the utilitarian materials of the building, prompted the design team to work with the existing conditions and establish a dialogue and tension between the new ordered layout and the existing, unordered building structure.

Organized around major and minor axes superimposed within the orthogonal shell, the layout is set up to control sight lines of interest and to promote a sense of procession within the sales area. Circulation by the customer through the 7,500 square foot retail facility is highlighted by controlled glimpses and partial views of spaces beyond, with their true nature not revealed until arrival. This sense of discovery creates an environment supportive of the intended retail activity.

Owner/Company
GILES & CO.

Architect/Designer
MOJO•STUMER ASSOCIATES

Contractor
HERBERT CONSTRUCTION

Photographer
FRANK ZIMMERMANN

When the design team was unable to use existing materials, a complementary palette of new finishes, including reconstituted crushed granite, steel cable, and terrazzo was incorporated. Hardwoods, stainless steel, and metal wire-mesh are used to accentuate special features of the space including the entry, structural columns, and display tables. The resulting blend of finishes, both old and new, creates a dynamic environment that complements the bold and adventurous merchandise.

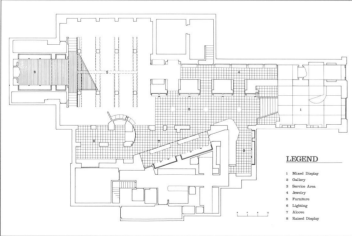

LEGEND

1 Mixed Display
2 Gallery
3 Service Area
4 Jewelry
5 Furniture
6 Lighting
7 Alcove
8 Raised Display

Great Pacific Patagonia

Apparel

Boston, Massachusetts

Great Pacific Ironworks worked closely with Bergmeyer Associates to find the right location and formulate the design for their new Great Pacific Patagonia store.

Manufacturers of climbing equipment and clothing, Great Pacific Patagonia was looking for an individual or freestanding building with historical character to emulate their own design philosophy. An exhaustive search led them to a two-story building in Boston's historic Back Bay. The requirements involved structural upgrades, the addition of a suspended mezzanine, and the project team's thorough understanding of how to fulfill the owner's desires within a challenging schedule and budget.

A construction schedule of 13 weeks, a budget of $95 per square foot, and an existing building full of unknowns quickly made the project team understand the owner's goals and produce efficient results.

Owner/Company
GREAT PACIFIC IRONWORKS

Architect/Designer
BERGMEYER ASSOCIATES

Principal-in-Charge
JOSEPH P. NEVIN

Lighting Designer
RIPMAN LIGHTING CONSULTANTS

Photographer
DAVID HEWITT

The 6,100 square foot building was stripped down and left with many structural components exposed including brick walls and ceiling joists. Natural and recycled materials, including recycled granite and refinished oak, were combined with new finishes, including commercial grade carpet and vinyl flooring.

Concentrating on the owner's desire to maintain the image of the renovated space, the designers combined the historical character of the building and its exposed components to create imagery that works with the company's philosophy.

G.H. Bass & Company Store

Shoes

Takashimaya Mall, Singapore

Owner/Company
G.H. BASS & COMPANY

Architect/Designer
**PARSONS + FERNANDEZ-CASTELEIRO,
PC ARCHITECTS**

Graphics/Merchandising
G.H. BASS & COMPANY

Contractor
**KINGSMEN DESIGNERS &
PRODUCERS PTE LTD**

Photographer
TONY LUAH

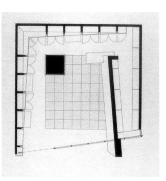

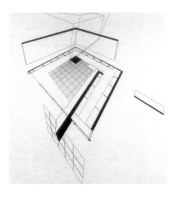

For the store design of an American shoe company in Singapore, Parsons + Fernandez-Casteleiro, PC Architects were empowered to define tradition for the young customer base of G. H. Bass & Company.

While the primary use of the store is for the seasonal display of shoe collections and daily retail activity, the architects were also asked to expand on the architectural vocabulary generated by the company's new regional showroom in New York City. The G. H. Bass & Company logo is displayed at several scales with a variety of materials including brass medallions and sandblasted glass. Custom wood display units and leather wrapped wall panels project the company's tradition of using natural materials

and attention to detail. The modular display units and furnishings are designed with built-in flexibility for organizing products and providing suggested retail applications for a changing merchandise base.

By mixing various grids on walls, floors, and ceiling, and shifting reference points by tilting wall and ceiling surfaces, the design allows for an assortment of displays including life-size photography and antique vignettes.

World Foot Locker

Athletic Footwear and Clothing

Dallas, Texas

An open and unobstructed interior plan for this 19,000 square foot sports store designed by Norwood Oliver Design Associates, Inc. includes a series of interactive venues that create a fast-paced shopping experience for customers.

Focal points designed to evoke a kinetic retail atmosphere include life-size mannequins frozen in motion on ramp-like structures to merchandise clothing. A playground-like basketball court complete with bleachers for customer seating includes programmed audio of cheering crowds, and an electronic scoreboard.

Owner/Company
KINNEY SHOE CORP.

Design & Planning
NORWOOD OLIVER DESIGN ASSOCIATES, INC. (NODA)

Lighting Consultant
JDA LIGHTING DESIGN, INC.

Contractor
TONY CRAWFORD CONSTRUCTION

Photographers
CUTTER/SMITH PHOTO INC.

Overhead, curved soffits with fiber-optic lighting reinforce the physical nature of the store and delineate traffic patterns. Interior structural columns are infused with similar energy and purpose as they taper from a thin base to a flared capital with inset mirrors. All elements of the store were designed to serve multiple uses including sweeping arcs of "invisible walls" for athletic footwear and multi-level circular seating platforms for displays and footrests.

World Foot Locker takes the inter-active merchandising theme to the to the fullest extent by creating an environment in which the customer and the merchandise are on the same playing field.

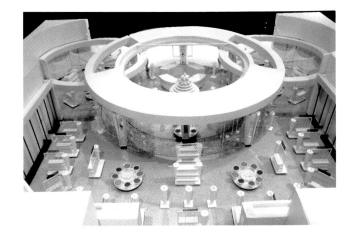

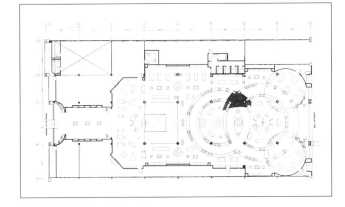

APPENDIX

Architecture & Design Firms

Bentley LaRosa Salasky,
Architects & Decorators
160 Fifth Avenue, #707
New York, New York 10010
Tel: (212) 255-7827
Fax: (212) 242-9117

Bergmeyer Associates
286 Congress Street
Boston, Massachusetts 02210
Tel: (617) 542-1025
Fax: (617) 338-6897

Clodagh Design International
365 First Avenue
New York, New York 10010
Tel: (212) 673-9202
Fax: (212) 614-9125

Dorf Associates Interior Design Inc.
106 East 19th Street
New York, New York 10003
Tel: (212) 473-9667
Fax: (212) 529-3250

Elliot + Associates Architects
6709 North Classen Boulevard
Oklahoma City, Oklahoma 73116
Tel: (405) 843-9554
Fax: (405) 843-9607

The Environments Group, Inc.
303 East Wacker, Suite 315
Chicago, Illinois 60601
Tel: (312) 644-5080
Fax: (312) 644-5299

Fitch
Porters South, 4 Crinan Street
London N1 9UE
United Kingdom
Tel: (071) 278-7200
Fax: (071) 833-1014

Florian • Wierzbowski Architecture, P.C.
432 North Clark Street, Suite 300
Chicago, Illinois 60610
Tel: (312) 670-2081
Fax: (312) 670-2102

Holey Associates
1045 Sansome Street, Suite 204
San Francisco, California 94111
Tel: (415) 249-4626
Fax: (415) 397-2857

HTI/Space Design International
860 Broadway
New York, New York 10003
Tel: (212) 254-1229
Fax: (212) 982-5543

The International Design Group
37 West 39th Street
New York, New York 10022
Tel: (212) 391-1162
Fax: (212) 575-3291

J.T. Nakaoka Associates Architects
1900 South Sepulveda Boulevard, Second Floor
Los Angeles, California 90025
Tel: (310) 479-4873
Fax: (310) 312-1005

Jensen & Macy Architects
241 Tenth Avenue, #1
San Francisco, California 94118
Tel: (415) 387-3692

The Jerde Partnership, Inc.
913 Ocean Front Walk
Venice, California 90291
Tel: (310) 399-1987
Fax: (310) 392-0898

Kirkpatrick Associates Architects, AIA
10801 National Boulevard
Los Angeles, California 90064
Tel: (310) 474-1616
Fax: (310) 475-0367

Kuwabara Payne McKenna Blumberg
Architects
322 King Street West, Third Floor
Toronto, Ontario, Canada M5V 1J2
Tel: (416) 977-5104
Fax: (416) 598-9840

Mojo•Stumer Associates
55 Bryant Avenue
Roslyn, New York 11526
Tel: (516) 625-3344
Fax: (516) 625-3418

Norwood Oliver Design Associates, Inc.
(NODA)
65 Bleecker Street
New York, New York 10012
Tel: (212) 982-7050
Fax: (212) 674-2302

Parsons + Fernandez-Casteleiro PC
Architects
588 Broadway, Suite 210
New York, New York 10012
Tel: (212) 431-4310
Fax: (212) 431-4496

Pompei A.D.
394 West Broadway, Second Floor
New York, New York 10012
Tel: (212) 431-1262
Fax: (212) 966-8659

Rockefeller/Hricak Architects
4052 Del Rey Avenue, Suite 102
Venice, California 90292
Tel: (310) 823-4220
Fax: (310) 823-3514

Rosenblum/Harb Architects
230 West 17th Street
New York, New York 10011
Tel: (212) 645-7474
Fax: (212) 691-6577

Schweitzer BIM
5499 West Washington Boulevard
Los Angeles, California 90016
Tel: (213) 936-6163
Fax: (213) 936-5327

Space Design International
311 Elm Street
Cincinnati, Ohio 45202
Tel: (513) 241-3000
Fax: (513) 241-5015

Tainer Associates, Ltd.
361 West Chestnut, Second Floor North
Chicago, Illinois 60610
Tel: (312) 951-1656
Fax: (312) 951-8773

Thane Roberts
1424 Fourth Street, Suite 502
Santa Monica, California 90401
Tel: (310) 458-9274
Fax: (310) 458-9351

TSL/Merchant Design Group
4465 Wilshire Boulevard, #100
Los Angeles, California 90016
Tel: (213) 938-3803
Fax: (213) 938-3216

Walz Design Inc.
143 West 20th Street
New York, New York 10011
Tel: (212) 229-2299
Fax: (212) 229-2398

Wormser + Associates, Architects
644 Broadway
New York, New York 10012
Tel: (212) 505-6962
Fax: (212) 477-0273

Zivkovic Associates Architects P.C.
100 Vandam Street
New York, New York 10013
Tel: (212) 807-8577
Fax: (212) 807-9575

Photographers

Jaime Ardiles-Arce
509 Madison Avenue
New York, New York 10022
Tel: (212) 688-9191

Paul Bielenberg
6823 Pacific View Drive
Los Angeles, California 90068
Tel: (213) 874-9951
Fax: (310) 675-3939

Tom Bonner
1201 Abbot Kinney Boulevard
Venice, California 90291
Tel: (310) 396-7125
Fax: (310) 396-4792

Brewster & Brewster Photography
429 West California
Glendale, California 91203
Tel: (818) 956-3717
Fax: (818) 956-0530

Andrew Bush
755 North Lafayette Park Place, #2
Los Angeles, California 92633

Tom Crane
113 Cumberland Place
Brynmaur, Pennsylvania 19010
Tel: (610) 525-2444
Fax: (610) 527-7529

Cutter/Smith Photo, Inc.
1645 East Missouri
Phoenix, Arizona 85016
Tel: (602) 274-5604
Fax: (602) 265-0779

Steven Evans
100 Broadview Avenue
Toronto, Ontario, Canada M4M 3H3
Tel: (416) 463-4493

Andrew Garn
85 East 10th Street
New York, New York 10003
Tel: (212) 353-8434

David Glomb
458 ½ North Genessee Avenue
Los Angeles, California 90036
Tel: (213) 655-4491
Fax: (213) 651-1437

David Hewitt
2587 Seaside Street
San Diego, California 92107
Tel: (619) 222-4036
Fax: (619) 222-2138

Christopher Irion
183 Shipley Street
San Francisco, California 94107
Tel: (415) 896-0752
Fax: (415) 896-1904

John Sutton Photography
8 Main Street
San Quentin Village, California 94964
Tel: (415) 258-8100
Fax: (415) 258-8167

Barbara Karant
Karant & Associates
400 North May Street
Chicago, Illinois 60622
Tel: (312) 733-0891
Fax: (312) 733-1781

David Lubarsky
30 East 20th Street
New York, New York 10003
Tel: (212) 505-1720
Fax: (212) 505-1727

Masao Ueda Photography
1534 8th Street
Fort Lee, New Jersey 07024
Tel: (201) 944-6931

Peter Paige
269 Parkside Road
Harrington Park, New Jersey 07640
Tel: (201) 767-3150
Fax: (201) 767-9263

Paul Warchol Photography
133 Mulberry Street
New York, New York 10013
Tel: (212) 431-3461
Fax: (212) 274-1953

Derek Rath
4044 Morre Street
Los Angeles, California 90066
Tel: (310) 305-1342

Sharon Risedorph
761 Clementina
San Francisco, California 94103
Tel: (415) 431-5851
Fax: (415) 431-2537

Francois Robert
740 North Wells
Chicago, Illinois 60610
Tel: (312) 787-0777

Bob Shimer
Hedrich Blessing
11 West Illinois Street
Chicago, Illinois 60601
Tel: (312) 321-1151
Fax: (312) 321-1165

Alan Weintraub
1832 A Mason Street
San Francisco, California 94133
Tel: (415) 553-8191
Fax: (415) 553-8192

Peter Williamson
1238 South Ashland Avenue
Chicago, Illinois 60680
Tel: (312) 733-6777
Fax: (312) 733-3083

Frank Zimmermann
P.O. Box 709
New York, New York 10159
Tel: (212) 645-4558

INDEX

Shops & Boutiques

A/X Armani Exchange 114-115
Anthropologie 36-39
Avant Garde 82-83

Banana Republic *(Beverly Hills)* 14-17
Banana Republic *(New York City)* 18-19
Barneys New York *(Dallas)* 30-31
Barneys New York *(Troy, Michigan)* 26-29
Belle Rose 110-113
Bergdorf Goodman Men 72-79

Caesar's World 46-49
Casakit Equippe 162-165
Christopher Hansen Ltd 130-131
CLIX 124-127
Communicate 108-109
Cornucopia 96-99

Dobson Telephone Company, Inc. 102-105
Doral Jewlers 70-71

Emporio Armani 132-135

Falabella 64-65
Felissimo 150-157

G.H. Bass & Company Store 174-175
Giles & Lewis 168-171
Great Pacific Patagonia 172-173

Hanna-Barbera 66-69

Joseph Abboud 140-147

Levi's Only 120-121
Looney Tunes U.S.A. 54-57

Mizani Uomo 84-87
MoMA Design Store, The 50-51
Mossimo Supply 40-45

Oasis 148-149
Ocella 166-167
Otto Tootsi Plohound 94-95

pH Neutro 100-101

Regional Transportation Authority Retail
    116-119
Rēvo 32-35
Roche Bobois 122-123

Salon Secrets 106-107
Sam Goody 20-25
Sara Sturgeon 158-161
St. Mark's Bookshop 88-93

Techsis 62-63

Urban Outfitters 58-61
Urban Outfitters Wholesale 136-139

Vasari 52-53

World Foot Locker 176-179

Architects & Interior Designers

Avila & Tom Company 14-17

Rafi Balouzian 158-161
Bentley LaRosa Salasky, Architects &
    Decorators 140-147
Bergmeyer Associates 122-123, 172-173

Clodagh Design International 150-157,
    162-165

Dorf Associates Interior Design Inc. 70-71

Elliot + Associates Architects 102-105
Environments Group, Inc., The 116-119

FITCH 64-65, 106-107, 166-167
Florian • Wierzbowski Architecture, P.C.
    108-109

GAP, INC. Store Planning 18-19

Holey Associates 32-35
HTI/Space Design International 50-51

International Design Group, The 120-121

J.T. Nakaoka Associates Architects 72-79
Jensen & Macy Architects 52-53, 62-63,
    84-87, 100-101
Jerde Partnership, Inc., The 20-25

Kirkpatrick Associates Architects, AIA 14-17,
    82-83, 130-131
Kuwabara Payne McKenna Blumberg
    Architects 148-149

Mojo•Stumer Associates 168-171
Musicland Group, Inc., The 20-25

Naomi Leff + Associates 114-115
Norwood Oliver Design Associates, Inc.
    (NODA) 176-179

Parsons + Fernandez-Casteliero PC Architects
    174-175
Pompei A.D. 36-39, 58-61, 136-139

Rockefeller/Hricak Architects 124-127
Rosenblum/Harb Architects 26-29, 30-31

Schweitzer BIM 40-45
Space Design International 54-57, 66-69

Tainer Associates, Ltd. 110-113
Thane Roberts 132-135
TSL/Merchant Design Group 46-49

Walz Design Inc 94-95
Wormser + Associates, Architects 96-99

Zivkovic Associates Architects P.C. 88-93

Lighting Designers

Apfel, David (HTI/Space Design International)
    50-51, 54-57
Architectural Lighting Design 132-135

Clodagh Design International 150-157,
    162-165
Craig Roberts Associates, Inc. 72-79

E.A. REA 120-121

Florian•Wierzbowski Architecture, P.C.
    108-109

Gordan, Gary (Gary Gordan Architectural
    Lighting) 88-93
Grenald Associates, Ltd. 14-17, 18-19

Holey Associates 32-35

JDA Lighting Design, Inc. 176-179
Jensen & Macy Architects 52-53, 62-63,
    84-87, 100-101
Joe Kaplan Architectural Lighting 20-25
Johnson Schwinghammer 26-29, 30-31

Kuwabara Payne McKenna Blumberg
    Architects **148-149**

Markus Earley Lighting **70-71**

Pascoe **46-49**
Carol Penfold **116-119**

Rand Elliot, AIA **102-105**
Ripman Lighting Consultants **122-123,**
    172-173
Rockefeller/Hricak Architects **124-127**

Schweitzer BIM **40-45**

Tainer Associates, Ltd. **110-113**
Theo Kondos Associates **64-65**

Walz Design Inc. **94-95**

Contractors

Anderson Construction **40-45**
A.P.C. Construction **58-61**

Braschi, Yuri **100-101**

Chicago Interior Construction Corp. **110-113**
Clyde Riggs Construction **102-105**
Coleman, Bob **84-87**
Columbia Art **70-71**
Continental Interiors **116-119**

Depreter, Paul **96-99**
Dinwiddle Construction **132-135**

Fisher Development, Inc. **14-17**
Floot Construction Design **120-121**

Glasser, Barry **108-109**

Herb Stewart Contractors **82-83**
Herbert Construction Company **72-79,**
    168-171
Hilton Construction Company **124-127**

J.I. Master Builders, Inc. **136-139**

Kajima International **150-157**
Kingsman Designers & Producers PTE LTD
    174-175

LJM Construction Inc. **88-93**

Middlesex Custom Interiors & General
    Contractors, Inc. **176-179**
Millworks Custom Fabricators Inc. **148-149**
M.O.S. Electrical **88-93**

Pacific Southwest Development, Inc. **20-25**
Pearce, Jan **62-63, 84-87**
Petrie, James **130-131**
Piazza, Anthony **162-165**
Porter Construction **122-123**

Richter & Ratner Contracting **26-29, 30-31**
Rocky Mountain Construction, Inc. **32-35**

Shabcon **158-161**
Shawmut Design and Construction **140-147**
Silver Rail Construction **94-95**

Photographers

555 DFM **118**

Ardiles-Arce, Jaime **72-79**
Aubry, Daniel **150-157, 162-165**

Balarin, Pablo **100-101**
Bielenberg, Paul **54-57, 66-69**
Bonner, Tom **58-61, 158-161**
Brantmeyer, Jorge **64-65**
Brewster & Brewster Photography **82-83,**
    130-131
Bush, Andrew **40-45**

Chen, Lucy **122-123**
Crane, Tom **36-39, 136-139**
Cutter/Smith Photo, Inc. **176-179**

Evans, Steven **148-149**

Garn, Andrew **94-95**
Giorgio Armani Corporation **132-135**
Glomb, David **124-127**

Hall, Steve **116-119**
Hedrich Blessing **102-105, 116-119**
Hewitt, David **172-173**
Hill, Christopher **166-167**

Irion, Christopher **62-63**

John Sutton Photography **32-35**

Karant, Barbara **108-109**
Karant & Associates **108-109**
Kezoh, Sue **118**

Linden, John **106-107**
Luah, Tony **174-175**
Lubarsky, David **96-99**

Masao Ueda Photography **70-71**
Masho Abe **120-121**

Paige, Peter **50-51**
Paul Warchol Photography **26-29, 30-31,**
    140-147

Ranson, Ashley **88-93**
Ranson Black Limited **88-93**
Rath, Derek **46-49**
Risedorph, Sharon **14-17**
Robert, Francois **110-113**

Shimer, Bob **102-105**

Waldron, William **18-19**
Weintraub, Alan **52-53, 84-87**
Williamson, Peter **118**

Zimmermann, Frank **168-171**

Acknowledgments

My sincerest appreciation goes to the many people who have both directly and indirectly contributed to the enormous effort in the production of this book.

Thank you to Steve Straughan, whose ten-year professional and personal association with me has redefined the term "team approach"...and to my valued office team including Russell Hatfield, Lisa Hunnicutt, Mark Hembree, Jennifer Thompson, Anthony Poon, Vince Jordan and, last but not least, Kana Higa—whose full-time devotion to this project was critical to its success.

For their encouragement, patience, and diligence to make this book the best of its kind, I would like to thank Mark Serchuck and Penny Sibal, and the art/editorial staff at PBC International: Richard Liu, Susan Kapsis, Francine Hornberger, Garrett Schuh, Deby Harding, Jami Hall, Christine Brako, and Lorine Bamberg.

Thank you to Kevin Clark for his foresight and faith in the "unknown" and for his assistance in contacts for the Call For Entries.

Thank you to Andrea Pappas whose wisdom and eloquence contributed to my Introduction, and to John Clendening who provided review and insight to the copy.

Thank you to my good friend Bruce Meyer, who has provided opportunities that I will never forget and whose nature is one for all to emulate.

And thank you to the following individuals for their personal contributions in assisting this work: Weldon Brewster, Don Fischer, Linda Gaunt, David Glover, Ali Hidari, Mary Lazzareschi, Thane Roberts, and Pavlov's Dog.

Most of all, thank you to my wife and partner Shaya whose global search for talented architects and designers during the Call For Entries stage resulted in the majority of the submissions herein, whose talent as a designer contributed to the editing, and whose support during late nights and long weekends created necessary inspiration and energy.